This Troubled Century

THIS TROUBLED CENTURY

Selected Addresses

of

Henry Louis Smith

Chapel Hill
THE UNIVERSITY OF NORTH CAROLINA PRESS
1947

Copyright, 1947, by
THE UNIVERSITY OF NORTH CAROLINA PRESS
PRINTED IN THE UNITED STATES OF AMERICA

Foreword

By RUPERT N. LATTURE

THE LIFE of Dr. Henry Louis Smith, which now covers a span of more than eighty-six years, has been extraordinarily rich and varied in accomplishment. His professional career has been marked by high attainments in the field of education and public affairs. As scientist and inventor he has won distinction and recognition. Notably he was the first American to take a Roentgen-ray photograph and the first to direct the surgeon by use of the X-ray during a surgical operation.

He is a member of the honor societies Phi Beta Kappa, scholarship; Omicron Delta Kappa, leadership; and Kappa Phi Kappa, editorship; and of the social fraternity Phi Delta Theta.

During the First World War Dr. Smith originated the time-balloon method of distributing widely all over Germany leaflets carrying Woodrow Wilson's appeal to the German soldiers and people against their war lords. In carrying out this project (kept a dead secret by the allies), twenty-five million message-laden red rubber balloons were scattered over Germany. This nation-wide propaganda was soon followed by widespread revolt among the Germans, the flight of the Kaiser, and the end of the war. To a group of distinguished visitors in the White House Woodrow Wilson, immediately after Germany's defeat, asked if any in the room knew the President of Washington and Lee personally and, on receipt of an affirmative answer, said, "Dr. Smith is a great man. He did more to bring the war to a close than any other living man," and in reply to a question by William J. Bryan the President explained the balloon method.

Following the war the Governor of Virginia selected Dr. Smith to be spokesman for a Commission authorized by the General Assembly of Virginia to present a bronze replica of the Houdon statue of George Washington to the government and people of England. On June 30th, 1921, the statue was unveiled in Trafalgar Square, where Dr. Smith made the presentation address to a host of appreciative listeners. An appropriate response was made by the Marquis of Curzon. Dr. Smith, during his visit to England, was acting for the Governor of the Commonwealth of Virginia, and by virtue of that fact he was accorded the courtesies of a visiting Crown Prince. Dr. Smith, Mrs. Smith, and the other members of the Commission were entertained by the King and Queen and by Lady Astor, Lady Markham, the City of London, the University of Oxford, and many others.

With a challenging and inspiring enthusiasm Dr. Smith has devoted his energetic life to opening the minds and stirring the hearts of young Americans. Tirelessly and effectively he has analyzed and interpreted the impact of science on modern institutions and values. He has issued clarion calls to young men and women to learn the truth, to live courageously, to mold the form and pattern of things to come. His progressive spirit, his unyielding loyalty to high standards in education and in public life, and his forthright manner of facing issues have thrust upon him a role of leadership in matters involving slum-clearance projects, temperance, racial justice, international-mindedness, and social and spiritual ideals. He is nationally known as an effective and eloquent public speaker.

Dr. Henry Louis Smith's father, the Reverend Dr. Jacob

Henry Smith, was a distinguished pulpit orator. Dr. Smith himself is one of four brothers who attained eminence in education and in the Christian ministry, all having their lives written in *Who's Who in America*. In 1881 he was graduated from Davidson College, winning medals in Greek, mathematics, and essay-writing. In 1891 he was awarded the Ph.D. degree by the University of Virginia and was the recipient of the Jefferson Society's gold medal in oratory.

From 1887 to 1912 he was successively Professor of Physics and Astronomy, Vice-President, and President of Davidson College. In 1912 he became President of Washington and Lee University, a position which will always bear distinction and honor as the only civil office ever held by General Robert E. Lee. Dr. Smith held this position until 1929, when he retired voluntarily with the title of President Emeritus. Since then he has continued lively participation in the affairs of Greensboro, North Carolina, his birthplace. He still appeals to the college-trained men and women of America "to perform the function of engines, not of box-cars." Thousands of his students and a host of other friends will welcome the publication of these addresses which contain so much of wisdom and inspiration.

Washington and Lee University

Table of Contents

I. EDUCATIONAL PROBLEMS   PAGE
1. The American College of Tomorrow 3
2. The Attitude of the Christian Scholar 14
3. The Transforming Power of Education 23
4. The Editor as an Educator 26
5. Robert E. Lee, the Educator 30

II. SOCIAL AND MORAL PROBLEMS
1. The Supreme Task of a Christian Democracy 37
2. Six Essentials of American Leadership 42
3. The Three Elemental Hungers 46
4. Driving or Drifting—Which? 51
5. Four-Square Manhood 55
6. Three Fundamental Choices 62
7. The Christian Home and Its Enemies 66
8. The Expanding Life 71

III. SCIENCE AND ITS INFLUENCE
1. The Culture Afforded by Scientific Study 79
2. Applied Science in the Civilization of Tomorrow ... 90
3. The Recent Marvels of Inventive Genius 95

IV. THE PRESENT-DAY CALL OF RELIGION

1. A Brief Talk on Religion 101
2. The Bible and Our Moral Standards 104
3. Tested by Fire 109
4. Luther before the Diet of Worms 119
5. A Twentieth Century Alliance—
    Business and Religion 129
6. "The Heavens Declare the Glory of God" 136

V. AMERICA TODAY AND TOMORROW

1. Virginia's Gift and Message to Great Britain 145
2. What Is the Matter with Christendom? 157
3. Some Things to Be Thankful for
    in the America of Today 164
4. The America of Today, Its Movements
    and Possibilities 170
5. The United States of Tomorrow 177
6. Our Social Progress in the Next Generation 187
7. America's Call for Lee Leadership 196

1

Educational Problems

The American College of Tomorrow*

IN ACCEPTING from the Board of Trustees, at the hands of their honored president, these symbols of an office enriched and ennobled by the great men whose memory is our most cherished heritage, I do so with an awe and solemnity which invest this simple ceremony with the sanctity of a sacrament. And as I face the unfolding future, which means so much to the University and to its new head, deeply conscious of human weakness and human infirmity, I desire to invoke for the incoming president and his associates the divine wisdom which guided Washington and Lee and Jackson in their mighty labors, the divine companionship which was their daily inspiration, and the divine blessing without which we build our house in vain.

Custom demands that an incoming president shall deliver an inaugural address. This may be an abstract educational discussion or an enunciation of his own principles and policy. Having spent my life in college teaching and administration, and having studied now for a whole year the assets and opportunities of this historic foundation, I have chosen the latter. With definite convictions, therefore, yet I trust with due humility, I desire to make of my inaugural a clear exposition of my preferred principles and program, not, be it distinctly understood, for any and every institution wherever located, but for the present work and present development of

* Inaugural Address at Washington and Lee University, May 7, 1913.

Washington and Lee, here among the green hills of the Valley of Virginia.

Our University, as all know, consists of two parts, harmoniously and organically united, yet pedagogically distinct: a professional School of Law with a most honored and fruitful history, and a typical, historic, residential, undergraduate American college. It is with special reference to the latter, though applying in principles to both, that I have selected as my subject "The American College of Tomorrow."

THE COLLEGE OF TODAY

As all wise development is a continuous growth, we cannot plan for the college of tomorrow without a preliminary survey of the college of today.

The American college of today, in the opinion of many leading educators, has been caught between the upper and the nether millstones and is losing its distinctive place and function in our educational system. The rapid development of our splendidly-equipped professional schools is steadily encroaching upon the four-year college period from above; while the American public high school, with its marvelous expansion and limitless resources, is absorbing the old freshman and sophomore years from below, till the junior college is becoming a well-established American Institution.

Not only is its place thus endangered, but the college itself is on trial and its work under fire as never before in our history. The recent magnificent development on our soil of the German-American university has made the graduate school the present home of American scholarship, research, and love of learning. Thus the college has been deprived of its former intellectual pre-eminence, and even those within its walls are everywhere lamenting the decay of its ancient scholarly ideals, the loss of intellectual virility among the dwellers on "Faculty Row," or the idleness and restless shallowness of the average undergraduate.

Meanwhile its outside critics openly declare that undergraduate life on the average college campus has become a unique combination of social loafing, childish frivolity, degrading dissipation, and strenuous athletics; where homeopathic doses of intellectual discipline, administered by discouraged physicians to unwilling patients whenever more important activities allow, are keeping up a mere pretense of old-fashioned hard study; where the conflict of ideals is so hopeless that the *maxima cum laude* graduate of the faculty is often the scorn of the campus, and the idol of the campus the dread of the faculty; where thousands of promising young Americans are taught to loaf and play ball but are fatally unfitted for the stern and relentless competition of modern business and professional life.

Truly these are weighty and specific charges. Yet let no one fear for the American college. Amid this Babel of accusing voices from without and within three stubborn facts challenge attention and demand explanation. First, our hard-hearted, cool-headed, far-sighted American business men are today investing more of their treasured millions in the American college than ever before. Secondly, our American parents are today entrusting more of their precious sons to these maligned colleges than ever before. And last and most important, somehow or other the graduates of these modern colleges, like their predecessors of a more rigid and studious era, still outstrip their non-college competitors in the race for life's prizes.

The key to this apparently hopeless tangle of opinions, facts, and theories is found, I think, in the fact that the American college is instinctively finding a new place and function. Against the despairing opposition of old-time college faculties, the spirit of the age, not content with transforming our political and industrial institutions, is resistlessly shaping our historic four-year college course to the needs and the call of a new social and civic order. The present seething ferment is not the chemistry of decay but the vigor of new wine bursting its outgrown and inelastic bottle.

The bane of our present educational system is the profesional pedagogue's belief that the chief end of man is study, and therefore the chief end of study is to prepare for further study. Acting on this theory the college has for generations chained and enslaved the high school, and is now in its turn chained and enslaved by the graduate school. Already is the American high school, in closer contact with the needs of the people, bursting its bonds and justifying its new-found freedom by an incredibly enlarged service. Not much longer, even in our section, shall its courses be determined and its standing rated by the further study of the tiny minority it prepares for college, but by the lifework of the many it prepares for citizenship.

Now let the American college also break her chains and have the moral courage to adopt a new ideal for her graduates and a new measuring rod for her processes. Her campus is no longer merely a training place for the learned professions; it is swarming with future American business men. Our complex and strenuous age finds little use for the dyspeptic hermit of the midnight oil who was once the laureate of the campus. To build a graduate fitted for efficiency and leadership in modern life the American college must prepare new plans and specifications.

The master-word of the eighteenth century was Liberty; its hero was the patriot. The master-word of the nineteenth was Knowledge; its hero was the scholar and the inventor. The master-word of the twentieth blends both into a richer and nobler ideal. It is Citizenship, the keynote of a new era, in which civic emphasis shall shift from human rights and privileges to human duties, when the power of knowledge and the gains of research shall be dedicated to the common good, when, we hope, fewer shall be called to die for their country, but many, nay all, shall be called to live for it.

THE AIM OF THE COLLEGE OF TOMORROW

In toil and conflict and disorder, in clamor and friction and misunderstanding, our age is shaping itself to this new ideal of co-operative citizenship and calling as never before for sane, broad-minded, far-sighted leadership. Let the American College of Today answer the call and furnish as her typical graduate, not the scholar equipped for further study, but the ideal Christian citizen equipped for life, trained not only to know, which is scholarship, and to appreciate, which is culture, but also to be and to do, which is citizenship; having a trained mind no less virile and vigorous than of yore, but working through a body equally trained to vigor and virility; not only learned but also resourceful and energetic; able to manage himself and other citizens; a citizen with a passion for righteousness and a self-sacrificing devotion to the public welfare.

HER NEW CENTER OF GRAVITY

To manufacture successfully this rare and complex product, the whole educational machinery of the college must revolve around a new center. For forty years, during our marvelous age of university building, we have been increasingly guilty of the moral sin and the educational folly of idolatry—the worship of Alma Mater. Her size and numbers, her endowments and architectural splendor, her fair name and growing renown—these have been made the end for which trustees, faculty, students, and alumni live and labor.

Surely if such idol-worship were anywhere so natural as to be excusable it is here at Washington and Lee. Yet even here let Alma Mater, with all her historic renown, be but the means to a greater end. Let her greatness be measured, not by the splendor of her own lineage or the reputation of her former sons, but by her present service to the individual student now on her campus. Around him let her whole organization, trustees, faculty, and equipment, revolve. Let his training, development, and inspiration be at once the aim and the measure of all her multiplied agencies and activities.

THE SCOPE OF HER OFFICIAL DUTIES

With her plans and processes adjusted to this new center, let the College of Tomorrow realize that the raw material entrusted to her molding hands is not the disembodied intellect alone, but the whole man, social, moral, physical, intellectual; separable in thought but not in growth; an immortal personality developing as one organic whole under the high-pressure stimulus of her classroom training and her campus ideals and activities.

With a cool head, a warm heart, and an unconquerable zeal, let teachers, administrators, and student leaders broaden the circle of their official duty and official responsibility to include not only classrooms and laboratories, but dormitories, boarding-houses, playgrounds, pleasure resorts, village streets, and campus loafing-places; not a student's recitations alone, but his health, habits, character, recreations, and social influence; not his recitation periods alone but the other nine-tenths of his time; not his intellectual training alone but the equally systematic and universal training of the body. And as these are all legitimate objects of college training, so expenditures for any and all these purposes are a wise and legitimate use of college funds.

HER AGENCIES

This broadening of scope and function multiplies the agencies which the College of Tomorrow must adopt, use, and control. These may be roughly grouped under six heads, and owing to their number and complexity must be merely enumerated, not adequately described.

First, the Faculty. For such work as we have outlined let us leave to the university her solitary explorers on the far frontiers of human knowledge and seek a type better fitted for our work. The ideal college professor should be, first, a man, human, magnetic, high-minded; second, a teacher, expert and inspirational, who will not tolerate shoddy work; third, a scholar, thoroughly acquainted with his subject and contagiously in love with it, but with his cutting edge of scholarship made effective by the momentum of a broad training and a strong personality.

Second, College Honors and Discipline. The whole system of college honors and discipline should be remodeled to fit the new ideal of college training. The solemn mockery of a faculty endeavoring to awaken ambition by crowning as the hero of commencement a graduate whom nobody wishes to imitate will be inconceivable when the new laureate combines the virtues of campus and classroom, and students and faculty unite in selecting him.

The government of most colleges is paralyzed by a strange mixture of semi-legal technicalities which tie the hands of the faculty, while giving an evildoer all possible legal privileges. These should be swept away by the open avowal that college government is neither legal nor punitive. Let all understand that no young man has any legal, moral, or inherent right to enter a college community or to remain in it.

As the father may at any time, in the exercise of his own discretion, withdraw his son or refuse to matriculate him, so the college authorities of an institution like Washington and Lee may grant or refuse matriculation as they deem best. They may also at any time terminate the connection of any student with the institution whenever in their judgment, and in theirs alone, such a separation is best for the student, for the institution, or for both.

With this assumption as its basis, college government should be preventive, corrective, sympathetic, and constructive; never merely punitive, and never hostile. With a personal kindness equaled only by its persistent inflexibility it will reject the unfit, eliminate the incorrigibly idle and the morally injurious, train these prospective citizens in organized self-government, and place as soon as possible all campus problems in their hands.

Third, College Athletics. The college which aims to train the whole man will realize the vast importance of the body, and will place its care and training on a par with those of the mind. The present one-sided and narrow development of college athletics, allowed through lack of faculty sympathy and control to run into many harmful excesses, has nevertheless been of inestimable value to college ideals and American manhood.

It should be organized as a subsidiary part of a universal, systematic, and compulsory program of bodily care and training. There should be also frequent medical and physical examinations designed to correct weaknesses, remedy physical defects, impart useful knowledge, train in physical morality, and build for every graduate a physique which will stand the long-continued pressure of modern American life.

Fourth, Social and Recreational Agencies. The fourth group of agencies to be taken over by the new college and guided, fostered, and utilized for its great end is the whirlwind of social, fraternal, religious, literary, and recreational activities which make the modern college campus a world in miniature. These under expert and sympathetic guidance have great educational value; without it they may work appalling mischief. Their number and complexity forbid detailed discussion, but their importance in molding student character can hardly be overestimated.

Fifth, the Campus Atmosphere. This is that invisible but all-pervading influence, the residuum of innumerable lives, experiences, customs, traditions, and associations, which is aptly called the campus "atmosphere." The fashions and traditional moral standards of a campus are almost as permanent as its buildings, and are generally more influential in making or marring the individual student than all the formal educational exercises of the classroom and the laboratory.

It will be the highest task of the new college to make this moral air, breathed hourly by every student, healthful and inspiring, and to wage relentless warfare against whatever vitiates or poisons it.

Sixth, Direct Faculty Instruction. A discussion of the formal instruction in the arts and sciences to be given by the college of tomorrow would exceed the time limits of an inaugural address. As this has heretofore been the controlling object of the outfit it is open to little criticism. The present opportunities for a student to gain such instruction in a modern college are little short of marvelous. Even the bitter critics of the modern college admit the genuineness and extreme value of the pearls. Their main contention is that they are fruitlessly and extravagantly cast before swine.

A frank and open avowal that the controlling business of the four-year undergraduate course is not the making of scholars but of all-round scholarly citizens may seem to some a dangerous experiment, imperiling what little scholarship is still left among our multifarious campus activities. To these I would commend a rather startling fact admitted by all who thoroughly know college life in America.

In spite of our learned faculties, our elaborate system of scholastic grades and scholastic honors, and our magnificent array of books and apparatus, prevalent student opinion on most American campuses rules that a student who enthusiastically uses these facilities is a hopeless "dig" or "grind" and calls the lowest passing mark, D, the "gentleman's grade."

It is as much the business of the farmer and is as essential to his success to prepare his seed-bed and keep it clear of weeds as it is to select the best seed and sow it with an expert hand. Let our college authorities realize that the habits and fashions, the "atmosphere" of the campus, determine the fruitfulness of every seed they sow, and therefore constitute an essential part of their official duty and responsibility. If this truth is taken to heart, the College of Tomorrow will not only be more friutful in the making and molding of men but will double the present output of scholars and investigators.

Such I conceive to be the aim, the methods, and the opportunity of the College of Tomorrow. Thus shall we rise to the high aim of our immortal post-war president, whose words of sublime simplicity I reverently repeat as I take up the task he laid down. "I shall devote my remaining energy to training young men to do their duty in life."

And where on American soil can an institution be found more clearly designed and fitted by an over-ruling Providence for such a service?

In her freedom to choose her own academic ideals, select her own raw material, teach with unfettered freedom, and uphold on her campus the highest standards both of scholarship and of conduct, Washington and Lee enjoys a unique and priceless privilege.

In her unrestricted field of service and of patronage, appealing to every class, every denomination, every state and section, she possesses an equally unique and priceless opportunity. In her location, her history, and her ennobling associations she is forever set apart from low aims and sordid labors to serve the things of the spirit.

Her seat is the Valley of Virginia, whose scenes of entrancing beauty have been hallowed by heroism and self-sacrifice. Her home is the town of Lexington, where the sacred dust of the great Puritan Captain awaits with confident faith the morning of the resurrection. Her campus was the home and is the burial place of that white-souled Cavalier who, uniting in his matchless character all ideals of Southern manhood, endowed her forever with the inspiration of his memory and the splendor of his example. From her cupola the Father of his Country looks down on the institution which he founded with his money and enriched with his incomparable name.

Long may these encircling mountains shut out for a while from our sons the noisy clamor of a petty world that, with their souls on fire, they may hear the voices of the immortal dead. Here at this sacred shrine, where the glory of the Old South burns in steady focus with the pure white light of an altar fire, may countless generations of young Americans learn the secret of power, the joy of service, the true meaning of greatness!

The Attitude of the Christian Scholar*

THE HIGHEST AIM of the Christian institution of learning should be to mold, inspire, and give to the world the Christian Scholar, the finest product of Christian intellectual training, in whom deep learning, wide culture, and highly-trained intellectual power are fused with glowing, contagious, personal religion.

Wherein does the Christian scholar differ from the learned Huxley, the cultured Voltaire, the brilliant and magnetic Ingersoll, the equally cultured unbeliever of any type? He has studied the same facts, in the same textbooks, perhaps under the same teachers; his mind follows the same logical processes; his speech and writing obey the same laws of rhetoric; and casual acquaintances may scarcely be able to distinguish one from the other. Yet the line of cleavage runs broad and deep between them, and each lives in his own world of thought, feeling, purpose, and aspiration.

This underlying essential difference is a difference of attitude, of inner relationship to himself, to his fellowmen, to nature, and to God. The traveler in the deep cañon and the explorer on the mountaintop see very different landscapes, though they may be studying and traversing the same mountain range. So the attitude or point of view of the scholar goes far toward creating the world in which he lives and is his own chief characteristic.

The cultured unbeliever, the typical man of the world, is

*Inaugural Address at Davidson College, May 29, 1901.

self-centered. He cultivates his faculties of mind and body that they may minister to his pleasure, popularity, wealth, or power. His purposes, however wide the range of his activities, are mainly concerned with Self. His attitude toward his fellowmen is mainly determined by the same motive. When useful to him they are used; when useless, ignored. When attractive to him they are loved and sought; when repulsive, shunned; when hostile, crushed.

To him nature is a gigantic engine, exquisite in its marvelous adaptations, awe-inspiring in its extent and power, but without heart or soul, without engineer or superintendent, rolling on its predetermined pathway of iron law, grinding to powder the puny schemes of man, crushing his cherished hopes in the dust, and leaving him, after a few years of vain toil and fruitless conflict, a handful of rotting clay, however costly the tomb that covers it.

Toward God the attitude of the irreligious scholar is one of uneasy ignorance, avowed agnosticism, cynical indifference, or open hostility.

Compared with the doubt, the darkness, the self-centered isolation of this traveler in the cañon, the Christian scholar walks a sun-lit path along the mountain tops, and sees both earth and heaven from a different point of view.

His body he regards as the tabernacle which enshrines a redeemed soul, to be cared for and reverenced as the dwelling-place of the Most High, and kept free from stain and defilement as befits its high vocation. Its natural appetites are to be refined and purified, its health and integrity preserved unimpaired, its animal passions controlled and sublimated, and all its capabilities maintained and developed because it is a temple of the Holy Ghost itself.

Toward humanity, poor struggling humanity, foaming out its own sin and shame like the troubled sea that cannot rest, he feels a divine pity and compassion. No earthly learning and culture can shut the gates of sympathy between him and his fellowmen. In every human being, whatever his debasement, he recognizes a brother, a soul for whom Christ died. There is no room in his heart for scorn, or cynicism, or cold indifference. The needs, the sorrows, the sins, the problems of others—these are ever sounding in his ears, calling him to the joy of service, the sublimity of self-sacrifice, the glory of consecration. By a divine compulsion his whole nature must answer the call and pour its choicest treasures, its holiest sympathy, into the lives of others.

To him the whole course of human history is but the unfolding of the complex and far-reaching plans of God. Ancient civilizations wax old as doth a garment and are laid away; empires reach their zenith and decay; persecution reddens the earth with martyrs' blood; the spirit of the age changes with every passing century; world leadership shifts from Persian to Greek, from Greek to Roman, from Roman to Anglo-Saxon, from Anglo-Saxon to we-know-not-what—yet through all and over all and guiding all the Christian scholar sees the mighty hand of God molding the world to His divine purpose. From this point of view, as from some mountain summit, his soul sees the end from the beginning, and is thrilled with the joy of coming triumph.

In the same spirit he examines the slow and steady progress of human thought. As the world's philosophy, conscious always of its unsatisfied hunger, grasping earnestly, though so often blindly, after truth, swings from one extreme to the other, the Christian scholar cannot give way to pessimism or despair. Above our petty human intellects he sees and feels the eternal Mind. To him the path of human philosophy is like that of some mighty ship, slowly beating her way into port against wind and tide. He knows that there is an almighty Hand at the helm, and that every tack, however long and divergent its swing, is bringing human thought nearer to the eternal Truth which finds its home in the mind of God.

So to all honest seekers after truth, in every area of human thought and experience, the Christian scholar bids Godspeed. The ardent physiologist, who resolves all thought and feeling into chemical action and reaction; the busy geologist toiling with pick and shovel, who thinks his fossils contradict the story of Genesis; the sincere evolutionist immersed in problems of heredity and genetics; the learned archaeologist examining the relics of long-lost civilizations and doubting the historic accuracy of the Old Testament—these the Christian scholar can never count among his enemies. He knows that all truth is one, that between God's Word in revelation and God's Word in nature there can be no real conflict; that to doubt this is to doubt the nature of God; that to *fear* the most searching investigation of God's Word or of His world is to be disloyal to truth itself as well as to the God of Truth.

The attitude of the Christian scholar towards God is never that of fear, distrust, or indifference. He bears to his Creator a combination of relationships, each one a separate wellspring of joy and strength, pervading, illuminating, and vitalizing his whole life. Though his mind has been enriched by years of study and his hair whitened by the frosts of age, to his Father in heaven he is a loving, trusting child. As to the tenderness of maternal sympathy the child brings every hurt for healing, every sorrow for comfort, every fault for forgiveness, every plan for approval, so the Christian scholar, whatever his rank or position among men, brings every sorrow, every want, every purpose to the loving heart of God.

Toward deity incarnate, the Word made flesh, his divine Elder Brother, his personal Savior, the heart of the Christian scholar burns with an all-consuming flame of personal devotion. This is his stimulus to action, his never-failing motive power, the ever-renewed inspiration of his life. Compared with its steady glow, the motives of the children of the world, love of gold, of learning, of power, are as the crackle of burning grass. In the pure white light of that love and loyalty all the finer growths of the spirit burst into bloom and fragrance; self-denial becomes a pleasure and privilege, daily sacrifice a daily joy, diffusive benevolence a law of his nature, and his chief end the glory of his Redeemer.

His intellect looks to the wisdom of God as its creator, its inspiration, and its guide. As an ardent student he interprets, with the joy of discovery, the revelation of God's thought in nature and humanity. As a faithful subject he strives to interpret rightfully arftd obey implicitly the commandments of his Lawgiver. As a loyal soldier, following the banner of his King, his heart is ablaze with the joy of sharing in the onward march of God's kingdom. He carries within him the consciousness of ever-present Divinity, sees everywhere the smiling face of God, and in life's tumult and conflict hears always that Voice which first brought order out of chaos.

Thus through life's pathway, whether rough or smooth, brightened by sunshine or swept by storm, the Christian scholar walks triumphantly as friend, companion, and faithful follower of his King. Over him falls day and night the glory of the world to come; and as the tidal currents swing to and fro with the changing moon, so his whole nature looks to the heavens and its currents ebb and flow in accordance with the will of God.

The attitude of the Christian scholar towards nature is based on his relation to its Creator. To him the material universe is the seamless garment woven about the form of God, revealing to every reverent mind His majesty and His love. The beauty of the outer world thus appeals to his innermost being. He sees it, feels it, revels in it as the manifestation of an inner divine harmony. Wherever his studies lead him, in the starry heavens, on lonely mountain top or desert plain or waste of ocean, he always sees before him a blaze of glory and hears the Voice saying, "Put off thy shoes from off thy feet, for the place whereon thou standest is holy ground."

To the trained intellect of the Christian scholar the material universe is the concrete thought of God. In its study he becomes the interpreter of its Creator and thinks His thoughts after Him. To the untrained, the uneducated, the unreflecting, whether Christian or unbeliever, our earth is but a vast monotony of rocks and soil, of grass and trees. Its mountains are but vast piles of earth and stone, its river valleys but unmeaning furrows in its surface. Its thousand variations of topography have no past history or inner significance. Its myriad voices are but a Babel of unmeaning noises.

Let a knowledge of its laws and processes but open the eyes of the mind, and every view of our ancient battle-scarred earth is an inspiration. To the Christian scholar and to him alone do earth and air and water reveal the secret springs of their multiplied activities, which are the wisdom and beneficence of a divine Creator.

Nature hails him as her true interpreter. To his attentive ear her thousand voices become at once articulate and intelligible. Every cliff and valley, every mountain plateau, every waste of desert sand, every seabeach and river cañon, is pregnant with meaning and bears testimony to a wondrous history. He looks back, with trained and reverent eyes, through an immemorial past, and watches the implacable struggle of fire and water for the possession of the new-formed world. He realizes the majesty of its Creator's power as His hand shapes our planet in the depths of space and with fire and flood, tidal wave and ice sheet, volcanic outburst and peaceful coral growth, prepares it for the abode of man. He catches inspiring glimpses of His wisdom and of His love as he watches the atmosphere slowly purified for his breathing, the harbors dug out for his future ships, the great plains fertilized for his crops, the coal and oil and iron stored underground for his use, and the whole world crowded with evidences of a Father's loving wisdom and foresight.

He traces the wondrous procession of strange plants and uncouth animals that peopled the forming earth, the monsters of the ooze and slime that fattened on the luxuriance of the young planet. He sees the continents forming one by one, the mountain ranges lifting their rocky summits toward the clouds, the oceans sullenly retreating to their foreordained limits, and the whole round earth thus fitting itself for future crowded nations and growing human brotherhoods.

It is when the Christian scholar thus follows in the creative footsteps of his divine Father, when his mind thus vibrates to the thunder of almighty power and draws back, with throbbing heart and reverent hand, the very curtains of Omniscience, that he rises above the miasmatic level of a petty world and breathes air fresh from the hills of God.

To the Christian scholar the glorious works of God illumine and illustrate His glorious Word. Would you realize the meaning of those words we carelessly repeat so often, concerning the minute care and watchful oversight of the Infinite Mind, that the hairs of our heads are all numbered? Then take the microscope and with the Christian scholar penetrate the world of the infinitely little.

A single drop of stagnant water swarms with countless thousands of invisibly small animals; yet to each of these He giveth his meat in due season as truly, as certainly, as carefully, as to the young lions that roar and suffer hunger. It is here that the Christian scholar learns, what most people never dream, that with God there is no great and small, no important and unimportant. The life of an animalcule is as carefully adjusted to its environment and as minutely guided and controlled as the growth and decay of a world.

Let me give one more instance of how scholarship uplifts

the Christian to a higher and wider vision of God in the study of nature. The untaught rustic may read in his Bible, perhaps with halting and difficulty, "The heavens declare the glory of God," and on his way home from the field, as he admires the star-spangled sky over his head, thinks he understands its meaning.

So the wren, flitting back and forth from his woodpile to the fence corner, admires the grass and daisies under him and might in bird language sing most heartily of the beauties of nature. What does he know, what can he dream, of the panorama unrolled beneath the eye of the eagle soaring in the depths of blue over his head? So the trained mind of the Christian scientist soars, intoxicated with sublimity, among the myriad wonders of the starry heavens.

Would *you* realize something of the meaning of the Psalmist's words? Then take the telescopic wings of light and travel among the hundred billion flaming suns that people the depths of space. Watch them all, forming nebulae, blazing suns, huge comets, tiny asteroids, planets crammed with life and satellites dead and withered; a vast company of revolving worlds, rolling in majestic silence along their appointed orbits, till the imagination faints under its load and the mind aches with insufferable sublimity. What perfection of order! What marvel of harmony! What majesty of power! What eloquence of grandeur!

Now, with intellect overwhelmed by the infinite, with heart suffused and trembling with breathless awe and adoration, turn from the God revealed in nature to His written message and tell me if you find no deeper meaning in those words of old, "The heavens declare the glory of God, and the firmament showeth His handiwork"!

Thus all Nature ministers to the Christian scholar. The stars light him on his way to heaven; the rolling earth carries him onward toward its Creator; the passing seasons as they come and go are molding his character into God's image; sweet influences from above give to his soul the very flavor of life and waken into music every fiber of his being; he stands ever on Mount Nebo and all the Promised Land lies before him.

Though, with his advancing knowledge, his idea of God is ever rising, splendor beyond splendor, till the thick-sown stars are the dust of His feet and frail humanity stands trembling at the thunder of His power; yet this God is his loving Father, bending from His throne to share every sorrow, every joy, every inspiration.

He cannot, therefore, walk through life with leaden footsteps nor sit down weary and discouraged on life's pathway. To him it is a royal highway along which a glorious company of prophets and heroes and martyrs and immortal leaders have walked with exultant footsteps on their way to glory. To him every spot on our fallen world may become holy ground, every human being is a brother, every human want a call to action, every earthly experience a steppingstone to heaven.

This, then, is the ideal Christian scholar, with the crown of a king upon his head and the wand of a prophet in his hand. Rich with the accumulated knowledge of our race, its science and literature and historic experience; richer still in the campanionship and friendship of God; he holds in one hand all the purest and loftiest pleasures of this beautiful world and with the other lays fast hold on eternal life.

Oh, Child of God! Oh, Glory's heir!
How rich a lot is thine!

The Transforming Power of Education

WE ARE just now ending two disastrous World Wars that have almost wrecked modern civilization. The two central powers that held it their right and duty to subjugate all other nations and to use every form of deceit, cruelty, and wholesale murder in doing so were Germany in Europe and Japan in Asia.

As a lifelong educator I wish to call the attention of every thoughtful American to the example Germany and Japan have been giving us of the transforming effect upon a nation's character and destiny of the kind of training given its young people.

Every Japanese child was thoroughly trained from babyhood to become a devout worshiper of his divine state and of its divine emperor, to believe that it was his right and duty to subjugate all the inferior races around him, that to accomplish this end every form of deceit, falsehood, and cruelty was a noble and praiseworthy act, and that death in such a holy cause was a glorious privilege reaping an immortal reward in being reborn as a Japanese baby but in a far higher station in life.

During the whole war every correspondent from the battlefields of the East has commented on the inspired courage of the Japanese soldiers and their utter disregard of cold, heat, backbreaking toil, and certain death in combating hopeless odds with sublime courage.

This is an almost awe-inspiring illustration of the transforming power of what we must call the religious education of their young people, lifting every soldier's hope and inspiration far above present toil and suffering toward a more glorious future. This is our educational lesson from heathen Asia.

Germany furnishes a second and much nearer example of education's transforming power. A half-century ago Germany held high rank throughout all Christendom for its higher education, its scientific research, its music, art, and literature. Traveling through Germany in 1891 on a bicycle tour of Europe, during the blazing heat of August, when nearly all the families were taking their meals outdoors, I was profoundly impressed by their family love and loyalty and especially by their tender care of their little children.

During the last two generations Germany has given to all her children from babyhood a Nazi military training even more universal and scientific than the Japanese, with the same self-glorification, the same ruthless subjugation of all opponents, and the same justification of falsehood, robbery, and wholesale murder.

The devilish cruelty of the once-Christian Germans after such educational training has shocked and appalled the whole world. Their educational program has not only uprooted all natural instincts of pity and sympathy, but has so affected the emotional nature that their soldiers take delight in torturing to death thousands of helpless prisoners of both sexes and all ages.

Let America, aiming to educate everybody, learn once for all this awe-inspiring lesson of the creative power of education when skilfully applied from early childhood.

These two modern examples prove that the instincts and ideals which we call character may be thwarted, modified, and even reversed by the training given a nation's childhood and youth. Let the American democracy of today, preparing, we trust and believe, to become the world-leader of tomorrow, take this educational lesson to its heart.

Two thousand years ago our Savior introduced into our

ever-warring world a new ideal of human civilization. He organized His personal followers into a self-propagating brotherhood, worshiping a God of Love, walking in the footsteps of a Prince of Peace, and believing with all their heart that love, not might, should be the impelling force in all human organizations.

It was the first experiment in genuine human democracy, holding that all men are equal in the eyes of God and have an equal right to eternal bliss in the loving democracy of a better world beyond the grave.

Even our professedly Christian nations have never realized or recognized our brotherhood with the black and yellow races of the earth, and in practically all our public schools and colleges, except in a few scattered localities, we have omitted in the last few years all regular training in religion and in morality.

Perhaps never in human history has the transforming power of education been so illustrated as in the case of Germany and Japan, and the absence of religious and moral training from our own public schools has led to such lawbreaking and youthful delinquency in the United States that all our jails and penitentiaries are today overcrowded, with all Christians everywhere lamenting our crime-ridden age.

Let every loyal American take to heart these lessons revealing the transforming power of education at home and abroad. Let us forward the movement to place Bible training in all our tax-supported schools and colleges, and let us liberally support and multiply our Christian colleges at home and abroad.

As the whole world is now organizing to prevent war among the nations, let us so transform our educational system that the trained leaders of tomorrow may bring about, not only a warless world, but a world of Christian brotherhood from one pole to the other.

The Editor as an Educator

THE REVOLT of a Christian minority against an ecclesiastical despotism four hundred years ago inaugurated a world-wide epidemic of democracy, of a growing recognition of the rights and the value of the lower classes.

This tidal wave of democracy has ever since been steadily transforming, not only our religious ideals and organizations, but our politics and modes of government, our commerce and industry, our home life and school systems, our dress, recreations, and social customs.

This movement toward universal democracy seems to have culminated in America, a modern mixture of all races, colors, and languages, settling upon and developing a new continent. In the United States every grown person, whatever his sex, religion, race, or character, regardless of his ignorance, vice, or ultimate purpose, can cast a ballot equal in its political power to the vote of the most highly-trained and far-visioned philosopher.

In other words, in the America of today, and still more in the America of tomorrow, Public Opinion creates, molds, and rules our American civilization. And our American civilization is becoming each year a mightier force in molding the world civilization of which it is a part.

Whoever, therefore, in this almost hysteric age of democracy, creates and molds American public opinion is the real teacher, creator, and ruler of our mighty Republic with its weighty world-influence.

As one whose whole life has been given to the formal systematic training of young Americans, let me prove to you that the Press is the chief educator and molder of the America of today.

We school teachers influence thousands; the editors teach millions. We teachers influence the young and uninfluential; the editors mold the opinions and activities of those who are doing the world's work and building the world's future. Our teaching and influence cover only the years of youth; theirs the whole life. We teach only a half-dozen hours a day, five days in the week, nine months in the year. Our newspapers and magazines teach every day in the week, every month in the year, every year in life's span from early childhood to the last days of old age.

Our students are often forced to their tasks; theirs are always voluntary students, eager and interested. Our textbooks are often dead languages, cold facts, abstract science; the editor deals with those facts, events, hopes, and fears that are thrilling the hearts of his readers. We teachers deal often with the dead past; the editors always with the living present. We teach a strictly limited circle of arts and sciences; the editor sweeps the whole gamut of human nature and traverses every avenue of human thought, hope, fear, and aspiration.

Let no one suppose that there is such a thing as colorless news, or the impartial reporting of daily occurrences. Every human experience is infinitely complex, with an infinite setting and background. No editor, therefore, or correspondent can give the whole picture of any current event. It is necessarily a case of selective transmission. The personalities of the various writers are like green, red, or blue glass. Each receives the white light but transmits its own color. Thus in this selective transmission even the news columns are steadily molding the judgments and opinions of every reader.

The newspaper editor has many complex functions, some of them highly important.

The first and perhaps the most valuable is to make every otherwise isolated reader a world-citizen, to put seven-league boots on his feet, a microscope at one of his eyes, a telescope at the other, and to bring him thus in close touch with every human interest in every part of the world.

His second glorious function is to lift with every issue ten thousand human lives above daily cares and petty local interests and to give to their minds and characters breadth and freedom, richness and inspiration, a wider outlook and a keener vision.

It is also his mighty and characteristic task to interpret our storm-tossed world to its inhabitants, to reveal to the individual and to his country what place each holds in the marvelous panorama of human development, to enable the patriot, the prophet, the statesman, the philanthropist to read the signs of the times, to lead whole communities, without friction or division or lost energy, to labor unitedly for the upbuilding of all.

The first half of the twentieth century has shaken to pieces the old world of yesterday and out of its shattered fragments is slowly and toilsomely creating the new world of tomorrow. The second half of this tempest-driven century is to see all mankind organized for world-peace and world-friendship and world-prosperity or rent into warring fragments preparing for a third world-war.

It is the newspapers and magazines of today that are determining the answer to this most weighty of all world-problems. Note the great movements of our formative age that are every day increasing their influence: widely diffused education, increasing religious toleration, efficient mail service all round the globe, the long-distance phone and the wonder-working radio, conferences and conventions meeting in every land, world-wide interest in social and political problems, with peace and brotherhood beginning to reign at home and abroad. All these are more and more making the twentieth century the age of the newspaper and magazine.

And is it any wonder that before this great Interscholastic Newspaper Convention, assembled in the Robert E. Lee Chapel of Washington and Lee University, in sight of that marvelous statue, that I find myself more and more wondering at the educational foresight of that great soldier, when, as President of Washington College in 1869, he organized and founded here the first collegiate School of Journalism in the United States.

Surely here was one educational statesman who could rightly read the signs of the times.

Robert E. Lee, the Educator

MY PRESENT DUTY and privilege is to present a picture of Robert E. Lee of which most Americans are strangely ignorant. General Lee was the hero of a hundred battlefields, the inventor of trench warfare, unmatched in defense, resistless in attack, whose fame as a military leader encircles the globe and grows greater with every passing year.

Yet, as a careful student of his life and career, I venture to declare that, when all the manifold results of his influence are finally summed up by heaven's unerring calculus and measured by heaven's unerring standards, the transcendent genius and lifework of Lee the Educator, the creative genius of a new industrial South, will outshine, outweigh, and far outlast all the more spectacular glories of his military career.

Lee as an all-American Progressive had outgrown slavery and manumitted his own slaves before 1861. As an ardent nationalist he hated the disruption of the Union as he did slavery, and never ceased his efforts against it till the Union prepared to invade and subjugate his native State, Virginia, and thus forced him to obey his deeper loyalty.

He was a far-seeing advocate of restricted and selective immigration in an era when America had opened wide her doors to the unfit of every land. Although a professional soldier, he regarded despotism as a regrettable military necessity, always lifted civic power above the military, and was a conspicuous exponent of self-government and social democracy, for church, school, and state.

It was due to his iron decision and all-powerful leadership that the Civil War ended at Appomattox and the nation was spared the endless horrors of guerilla warfare which his gallant associates urged upon him before his surrender.

That the whole South a single generation later could so nobly lead the nation in fighting and dying under the old flag was due more to his shining example and patriotic efforts than to any other leader North or South during those awful years of Reconstruction with its strifes and hatreds.

When his starved and ragged handful of heroes surrendered at last to overwhelming forces, the greatest soldier of his time suddenly found himself without a profession, in the midst of a bankrupt and devastated land. Worn by toil and hardship, his wealth gone, his stately home confiscated, with a helpless family dependent on him for daily support, he was at once offered wealth and a home in England, wealth and high military position in Egypt, and at home a huge salary as the nominal head of a great business enterprise.

Meanwhile the Rector of the Board of Trustees of Washington College, his borrowed coat and borrowed horse and borrowed money for traveling expenses typifying the desperate poverty of his war-wrecked and bankrupt institution, rode across the Blue Ridge and urged the idol of the South, on a salary of fifteen hundred dollars, not a dollar of which was yet in sight, to bury himself in a mountain village, forty miles from the nearest railroad, and to undertake the herculean task of rebuilding the fortunes of a bankrupt college, of preparing the young men of the South to solve the problems and bear the burdens of their harassed and stormy times, and of thus reuniting the severed sections of the Union under the old flag.

It was a momentous choice. On one hand was rest, rest for his worn body and his worn mind, ease and wealth and comfort and medical care not only for himself but for those he so dearly loved, a peaceful evening for his stormy life.

On the other hand were ceaseless labor and daily worries, painful and conscientious adjustment to a new and exacting sphere of duty, an unending struggle with grinding poverty and lack of equipment and resources, no possible prospect of rest, ease, wealth, or peace, till he found them all in the grave.

His prompt affirmative decision was the sublimity of self-renunciation and consecration at the combined call of duty, ability, and opportunity. With an educational statesmanship more amazing than his military genius he rapidly transformed an ultra-classical college of the nineteenth-century type into a training school of civic and industrial leadership fifty years ahead of his age.

He at once introduced the elective system in place of the former fixed curriculum, organized student self-government instead of exclusive faculty control, the "honor-system" in all tests and examinations, and an organized Y.M.C.A. of the national inter-denominational type.

Never had such a leader of men given himself to an institution of learning. One year was spent studying the institution's historic past, its present problems, and especially its possible future service to a wrecked and prostrate land whose social and industrial system had been suddenly annihilated. Then, with daring progressiveness, with consummate ability, with resistless and untiring energy, the reconstruction began.

To the traditional undergraduate work in Latin, Greek, mathematics, and philosophy were added in rapid succession Departments of English, Modern Languages, Applied Chemistry, and Natural Philosophy; and each year thereafter a thoroughly planned professional school was presented to the Board of Trustees and adopted by them: in 1867 a School of Law and Equity to furnish the new era in the South with highly-trained lawyers and legislators; in 1868 a School of

Civil and Mining Engineering to rebuild the wrecked South; in 1869 a practical and theoretical School of Journalism to furnish the new era with trained leaders of public opinion; and in 1870 a thoroughly-planned School of Commerce and Business Administration for the industrial and economic leadership of the new industrial South. These last two were, as far as I can ascertain, the first collegiate schools of this type or name in America.

Thus in five formative years this former Superintendent of West Point worked an outstanding miracle in the history of American non-military higher education. Thus, in these short years of poverty and wreckage, he transformed an ancient classical college into a twentieth-century university of practical training.

With the magic of his name and energy he gathered students, teachers, endowments, and equipment on Washington's educational foundation; saturated the institution with his spirit; fixed, I trust for all time, its campus traditions of chivalry, courtesy, and personal honor; and then, worn out by his incessant labors, fell suddenly at his post, and bequeathed to it for all time his matchless example, his sacred dust, and his incomparable name.

Thus, like his divine Exemplar on the hills of Galilee, he sacrificed his mortal life that his life-work might thus become immortal, and taught the world the glory of self-renunciation, of wholehearted Christian consecration, of fidelity to the heaven-sent duty of the hour at whatever cost of personal sacrifice.

Would God such a spirit, such dauntless moral energy, such daring progressiveness, such educational statesmanship, were leading the storm-tossed and bewildered America of today!

11

Social and Moral Problems

The Supreme Task of a Christiam Democracy

TILL THE COMING and mission of Christ inaugurated a democratic form of brotherhood in the world the only method of human government evolved was autocracy in some form. The forms ranged from absolute despotism on the part of a single tyrant to modified monarchy under a parliament, itself largely hereditary. All these forms were what may be called government from above.

The United States, after winning its freedom from Great Britain, originated a democratic form with no hereditary titles or offices, modeled largely after the regular government of certain Protestant denominations which had settled its area. The steadily rising level of comfort and human welfare in the United States has popularized democracy in Europe and America, till the leading civilizations of the world are today largely democratic.

The two World Wars that have desolated the whole world during the first half of the twentieth century have been largely a conflict between the ideals and followers of democracy and the ideals and subjects of world tyranny.

It now seems probable that in the rebuilding of our wrecked world-civilization the triumphant forces of democracy will have the largest share, although many of the political and social forms of democracy will be materially modified.

Unquestionably government of the people, by the people, and for the people will, however slowly, ultimately envelop and transform our whole world-civilization. Let us try to answer a few very important questions as to this newer and happier era which, we trust, our war-torn world can now anticipate.

What will be the status of education in that democratic era? What social and legal position will the boys and girls of America occupy in the coming era? What great ideas and new truths now shaping themselves in the crucible of human thought will then determine the attitude and duties of American manhood and womanhood toward American boyhood and girlhood?

To anticipate these ideals and duties is to prepare ourselves for fruitful leadership in the World of Tomorrow. To recognize them is to clarify our vision of duty. To put them into swift execution is to hasten the coming of that better day.

For these good ends we must recognize and apply five great truths of any successful democratic civilization. These are:

First: That the children of a nation are at once its most valuable asset, its chief source of undeveloped power, and its most fruitful field for unlimited investment.

We invest billions in American stocks and bonds for a beggarly five or six per cent which, if invested in American boys and girls, would enrich us beyond imagination. No unyoked cataracts in our mighty rivers have such stores of potential energy, no rich alluvial plains such promise of abundant harvests, no undiscovered mines such inexhaustible treasures as the undeveloped boys and girls of America. Our most stupendous blunder in the past has been to undervalue them; our greatest present crime is our neglect of them; our most suicidal stinginess is to make inadequate provision for their health and happiness and right training for the duties of their future citizenship.

Second: That the right training of all its future citizens is the supreme task of a Christian democracy, the test and measure of its civilization, the highest and most fruitful of all its manifold activities, its most complex and difficult problem, its most inspiring and limitless opportunity.

Let but one single generation of American boys and girls be rightly trained in body, mind, and spirit, in knowledge and love and unselfishness, and all the knotty problems of our American life, social, economic, and political, would be far on the road toward complete solution.

Let the training of but one generation be wholly neglected, and our American civilization, losing its art, science, literature, and religion, would be far on the road to primeval savagery.

The right training of the young is the spiritual reproduction of the race, the blooming flower of a nation's civilization, the most accurate test of its wisdom and culture, the highest and most fruitful form of all human activity.

Third: That the training of the intellect alone is fatally inadequate for a self-governing democracy. The heart must be trained with the head in the Christian principles of love and justice, of sympathy and unselfish service.

There is nothing theological, ecclesiastical, or sectarian about these laws of right living. They can and should be taught in every school in America from the kindergarten to the university. If any of us, in our zeal for book-learning, have believed and taught that mere knowledge, intellectual training, inventive genius, are the adequate solution of a nation's problems, let the tragic deterioration of German character at the very time when she excelled in science and inventive genius stand as a gigantic object lesson warning our more youthful nation from this seductive pathway to national ruin.

Fourth: That the substitution of the Rule of the Many for the Rule of the Few will inaugurate a worse tyranny than any we have so recently overthrown unless the Many are trained in both knowledge and character to use their power wisely and justly.

This is the darkest cloud on the world's horizon today; this is the fear that grips the stoutest heart: that the blood-bought rights and liberties we have so painfully accumulated through centuries of blood and tears shall be trampled under foot by the ignorant and unthinking.

From this impending calamity nothing can save us but the swift diffusion of love and justice and enlightenment and Christian brotherhood among the Many before the triumph of democracy places all worldly power in their hands. This is the appalling crisis, this the huge task, and this the heaven-sent and sublime opportunity of all the teachers and preachers and parents and social leaders of our storm-tossed era.

And for the comfort and inspiration of all these workers among our young people let me add:

Fifth: That the fifth characteristic of the new era will be its frank recognition of the greatness of their task and the glory of their service.

When our giant democracy emerges from its youth-era of inexperience and experimentation, when our hero-worship shall have become sane and wise, when love and co-operation shall be the law of American life and unselfish service the measure of American greatness, then it will be universally recognized that the true leaders and makers of the nation are not its millionnaires nor its railway magnates nor its politicians but those who mold and train and inspire its boys and girls.

Let all of us, then, who are at work among the young people of America go back to our fields of labor with our vision clarified and broadened, our working program made wiser and more definite, and our hearts on fire with the glory of our great task.

Then will our zeal kindle the hearts of others in ever-widening circles; then will daily drudgery become a daily pleasure; and thus shall we hasten the coming of that new era when every American child shall be the object of a nation's care and love.

Six Essentials of American Leadership

A Heart-to-Heart Talk with Young Americans in School or College

In "getting an education" you are on the most direct road to American leadership, and this means to a high place among your fellow-Americans, whether you are distinguished by great wealth, high political place, or leadership in education, business, journalism, authorship, or any other line of activity. Remember from the beginning that in the America of today and still more in the America of tomorrow, every kind of leadership must be won and not forced. The day of the despot in business or politics or religion belongs to the past.

I wish to describe six characteristics or qualities, every one of which is a long step toward becoming a "big success" in the competitive whirlwind of American life. Burn every one of these six essentials into your memory, your heart, your will power, your backbone.

The first of these six characteristics which I will mention is steadfast home loyalty, that ever-increasing love and regard for his home-folks which no school playgrounds, nor college campus, nor prep-school dormitory is ever allowed to dim or cool or weaken. Let no new environment, no school or college "gang," no new fashions of speech or dress or behavior, ever lead you to look on that absent father or mother as rather out-of-date, an old-fogy whose wishes and ideals may be wisely laid aside.

Enrich your adolescent life with many new friendships, new loyalties, and new ideals, but never allow them to dim or weaken your home loyalty.

The second element of all-round American character is high-minded individualism; and nowhere is this harder to develop and maintain than amid the close-knit swarms of young Americans in the imitative, crowd-worshiping stage of adolescence.

If you have the habit of agreeing with your special "gang" of intimate associates, if you are proud of always "keeping up with the procession," if you can't bear to say or do anything which will make you less popular, if you cannot decide on a suit or new dress till you find out just what your crowd is getting, let me assure you that you are preparing to play "second fiddle" in all future concerts, to start with eager obedience whenever the "boss" says "Go." You'll be a life-long follower, never a genuine leader.

The crying need of our American civilization today is not more second-rate, gang-following politicians but more trained and high-visioned leaders who can swing the crowd their way.

The third element of American leadership to be zealously developed before maturity has made such development very difficult is a winning personality. This means that magnetic fraternalism which influences other people; which so tempers and sweetens a leader's aggressive individualism as to win enthusiastic followers.

If you find yourself forming the habit of suspicion, of jealousy, of envy; if you are becoming unable to rejoice in the success or good fortune of your associates; be warned in time. Resolutely alter and sweeten those habits and attitudes, or you'll find yourself traveling in low gear on the road to leadership.

Here is the double message of the second and third elements of successful manhood in a single pregnant truth. Aggressive individualism and magnetic gang-leadership joined in a single personality—this is the magic twin key that opens every door to power and wealth and high position in the America of today.

The fourth element of future success is habitual intensity, of will, of purpose, of effort. Every path to success is today an uphill road. Every approach to every desirable goal is blocked by determined opponents. Every victory in every line of American activity must be fought for and won.

If, in this formative period, you are allowing yourself to form habits of postponement, of tardiness, of hesitation, of indecision, of half-hearted work and half-done jobs; in other words, *if your personal engine is not developing driving power,* you are a foredoomed failure, not in college studies and school activities only, but in the competitive warfare of American life.

Let me urge you, therefore, to form the fixed habit of highpowered intensity, of white-hot determination, of running your personal engine with such a driving power that no uphill road or thickstrewn obstacles can annul or defeat.

The fifth key to leadership and success is unflagging persistence, the never-say-die habit of mind and action that never works by fits and starts or yields to discouragement in the face of opposition.

In the grind of your daily studies, in overcoming your weaknesses and besetting sins, in opposing your lower nature and your animal appetites, in fighting your daily enemies within and without, never forget that unflagging, undiscouraged *persistence* is the straight road to victory.

The sixth characteristic of ideal manhood and womanhood, the most permanent of all your possessions, that touch of the divine that allies man with the infinite and eternal and lifts him above the petty and the transient, is moral character, high-minded morality and self-control in thought and word and action.

The Southern ideal of culture and character is that marvelous mixture of the stern morality of the Puritan with the social charm of the Cavalier that lifted Robert E. Lee to his unique place as the highest embodiment of all-American manhood which our Anglo-Saxon civilization has yet produced.

Let every loyal American citizen write these six characteristics of successful leadership on his mind and memory, sink them deep in his heart, let them flower in his daily life: a steadfast and unchanging home loyalty, which no environment can weaken; a strong and courageous individualism, which never yields to the clamor of the crowd; a loving fraternalism, which links the crowd to its magnetic leader; an intensity and persistence that unite to ensure victory on every American battlefield; and a high-minded morality that links every quality and purpose and effort with the eternal and divine. These constitute the open gate to future leadership in the American empire of the Twentieth Century.

The Three Elemental Hungers

A Frank Talk to Young Men

IN ORDER that man may maintain his individual existence, preserve the continuity of his race, and develop an ordered civilization, the all-wise Creator has endowed him with three elemental, universal, and necessary instincts or hungers.

These are bodily appetite, or Food-hunger; the mating instinct, or Sex-hunger; and the love of individual possessions, or Property-hunger. These divinely implanted and universal instincts are not only necessary to the perpetuation of the human race and its civilization, but are in themselves essentially wise and beneficial. When rightly used they immeasurably increase the happiness and welfare of the race.

Each of these instincts is not only natural and divinely created, but in no sense sinful or degrading. Each of them, when refined, controlled, and spiritualized, may prove to be the red clay soil out of which will grow into blossom and fragrance the fairest flowers of hospitality and chivalry, of the noblest personal character, of social charm, and of Christian brotherhood and self-sacrifice.

The misuse of these elemental instincts, or their uncontrolled mastery of the human animal, unchains every devilish instinct, undermines and destroys the home and the home-circle, turns human beings into beasts of prey, fills our jails, hospitals, and insane asylums with human wreckage, and extinguishes every trace of the divine in human behavior.

Let us briefly recall and examine these three elemental hungers, leaving each of us to think the matter through, to reach unshakable convictions of personal danger and of personal duty, and then, with iron resolution, to transform these fixed convictions into daily habits and personal self-mastery.

The first of these instincts is Food-hunger, the body's instinctive craving for food and drink.

This craving is instinctive, universal, honorable, wisely implanted, and necessary to human existence. It is man's greatest incentive to fruitful activity and daily labor. With wise control and proper gratification, bodily appetite gives a human being growth, health, grace, vigor, happiness, long life, and freedom from a thousand pains and weaknesses.

When idealized and refined, this necessary habit of feeding the body becomes the chief social bond of the home circle, the source and inspiration of hospitality and generous friendship, of self-forgetful social intercourse. Eating food together, thus spiritualized, becomes the very pledge of mutual love and loyalty and of self-forgetting fidelity.

This same bodily hunger, if set free and unguided, is like the blessed hearth-fire turned loose to devour the home and the home circle. Uncontrolled animal appetite creates the glutton, the drunkard, the dope fiend, the raving maniac, the devil in human flesh.

The wild beast, snarling over his prey, attacking all who approach, untamed, selfish, brutal—this is the human being enslaved by drink or dope, unable to control his natural appetite for food and drink.

Let every young American approaching maturity, and every American man and woman on life's arena, in this whirlwind age of self-indulgence, learn to control and spiritualize his bodily hungers lest they control and brutalize him.

The second of these divinely-implanted instincts is the Mating Instinct between men and women on which the preservation of the human race depends. As Food-hunger maintains the life of the individual, so Sex-hunger is the divinely-chosen method of preserving the life of the human race. Without it our human family would soon become as extinct as the mammoth or the mastodon of ancient geologic eras. There is no human instinct more imperious than love between the sexes, and none more wisely ordained for the happiness and welfare of the race as well as for its perpetuation.

Though rooted in the rank red clay of our animal nature, the mating instinct is not in itself degrading or sinful or in the least unworthy. It may develop and flower into all that is richest and highest and sweetest in manhood and womanhood. When rightly controlled and spiritualized it is the fruitful source of home joys and the home circle, of parental love and filial devotion, of chivalry and poetry, of music and art and romance, and of spiritual hope and faith and aspiration.

When uncontrolled and unguided this animal instinct tramples all human culture and courtesy and self-restraint into the mire of man's brute nature. When warped or psychologically perverted, it makes a human being a degenerate, more loathsome than any beast, more cruel than any imagined devil of the pit.

It cripples the human body with the horrible venereal diseases, whose fatal effects on home and children and innocent womanhood, now largely hidden from public knowledge, make the much-advertised ravages of tuberculosis seem almost negligible. These diseases are the overwhelming and universal curse of modern civilization.

Very fortunately for humanity the former veil of secrecy held over them and their effects by the medical profession and the public generally is now rapidly disappearing, and in every highly-civilized land the government is laboring to extirpate these two destructive diseases. But they are still filling our whole land with human wreckage, blighted hopes, and blasted homes.

Let me warn every young American that at present the only really safe plan for life is for each sex to marry a virgin mate, thus founding an ideal home for the rearing of unblighted young Americans to become leading citizens of the better America of Tomorrow. Let this be your resolute purpose, your cherished ideal.

The third of these elemental and universal instincts is Property-hunger, the desire of personal ownership, the passion for acquisition. This is the motive power that drives the vast and complex machinery of the modern industrial world of individual and corporate labor.

It is the underlying basis of our modern capitalistic civilization, with its multiplied organizations and activities. When wisely guided and controlled, it preserves the treasures of the past, inspiring each generation to add to the accumulation, thus always tending to banish poverty and to make each generation happier and more comfortable than the preceding. This is its effect when rightly guided and controlled by justice and morality and glorified by love and brotherhood and public spirit.

When uncontrolled or perverted this desire for other people's property poisons and degrades individuals and whole nations. It is the most appalling problem of modern civilization, filling every land with policemen and detectives, with jails and penitentiaries, and an elaborate system of courts and trials and lawyers. It everywhere forces the weaker to the wall and grinds the life out of helpless women, defenceless lower classes, and dependent children.

When whole nations turn robber, conquering and robbing and enslaving weaker nations to enrich themselves, it compels other nations to combine for mutual self-defence, till the whole world is given over to warfare and its manifold attendant miseries.

As each individual government must organize to protect the individual citizen against theft and robbery, so it seems necessary for the whole world to organize itself into a World State for the protection of individual nations against each other, compelling international quarrels and disagreements to be settled before courts of international justice rather than, as heretofore, on fields of battle.

These are the three elemental hungers on whose moral and legitimate satisfaction human happiness and prosperity so largely depend, Food-hunger, Sex-hunger, and Property-hunger. Let every citizen, old and young, learn so to use and control them as to increase his own and his neighbors' happiness and comfort and welfare.

Driving or Drifting — Which?

OUR JOURNEY, from the cradle to the grave, across life's restless sea is a never-ending movement. Yet some life-travelers seem urged hither and thither by every varying wind and current, while others are evidently moving toward some fixed destination.

Any observation of the many life-travelers around us will convince us that on the wind-swept and storm-tossed sea of American life the mariners may be roughly classed as either Drivers or Drifters. And anyone watching young Americans in school or college will soon learn that the mode of progression, whether driving or drifting, is crystallizing as a fixed habit during the formative period of youth.

Let me say, therefore, to every young American: Your daily and hourly routine, your habits of work and recreation, your aims and attitudes and ideals, are all steadily crystallizing into lifelong permanence.

Your future life-career, as a success or failure, isn't simply a matter of intellect, or of brain power, or of education, or even of moral character. Some of our ablest men intellectually, some with the finest college training, many of irreproachable character, never reach any harbor of success, but seem to be lifelong drifters on life's troubled sea.

The goal you will reach amid life's treacherous currents is largely a question of your inner motive power; that is, whether in your formative youth you formed the habit of driving or of drifting.

Let us, therefore, examine with both mind and heart the underlying difference in daily life between a Driver and a Drifter.

The big difference, underlying and controlling all the rest, is the possession or the absence of personal motive power.

The life-craft of a Driver has an engine which generates its own propelling power. Thus equipped he can aim at and reach a desired port regardless of wind or tide or opposing currents or the routes chosen by other ships.

To the Drifter such self-determined movement toward a far-off goal is impossible. His craft is at the mercy of every wind that blows and every current that flows. In other words, a Driver controls his environment and hence his movement. To a drifter the environment is all-powerful.

Through inherited peculiarities or weaknesses of mind or of body or of temperament very many human beings lack the faculty of energetic constructive leadership. They are born without this inner motive power, this power of decision and initiative and personal magnetism. If thrust into important executive positions they soon become failures.

Such men or women may become very successful and happy subordinates. They should be very diligent, loyal, and high-charactered. Let them be sure to attach their non-engined craft to wisely-selected organizations or leaders, and do their work in the world with the comforting assurance that for carrying the world's goods to their right destinations the freight or passenger car is as essential as the locomotive, the loaded barge as the towboat.

A driver without conscience or character not only wrecks himself but all his followers. Such citizens become our leading criminals of every type, often lowering the moral level of a whole city or state before their arrest or punishment. A drifter who lacks moral character is almost sure to be led astray. Especially is this true of the vast number of drifters who have no settled vocation or location in the business world.

Such unattached drifters are the fertile recruiting ground for the vast army of beggars, hobos, slum dwellers, and criminals of every type, a floating population which constitutes today the leading unsolved problem of our American civilization.

Your urgent duty, your wisest and most profitable line of habit formation, your straight road to happiness and success, is, therefore, two-fold.

First: Learn to be an ideal and highly successful subordinate, with respect to your parents, your teachers, your officers or directors. Whether your field of action is the home, the church, the school, the playground, or the summer camp, see to it that you cultivate and reveal fixed habits of loyalty, diligence, punctuality, and wholehearted faithfulness.

Whether your future vocation is to be nation-wide leadership or some subordinate's position in a village store, these habits in your early days will not only win for you friendship, esteem, and reputation, but will carry you to the highest position in reach of your abilities. Cultivate them, therefore, every day, with never-flagging zeal and persistence.

Second: Endeavor from your earliest childhood not to be merely yielding and obedient but to cultivate the habit of furnishing and developing your own motive power. Request your parents to give you an alarm clock and watch you with its help get to breakfast and to school on time every day with no reminder from them.

Let the same self-originated motive power carry through your daily routine of the bathroom, the dressing-room, your regular home duties, and your study periods. Let your duties of every kind, especially those which are hard and hateful, be attacked and conquered of your own volition with the joy of battle in your eyes and heart.

Even in a subordinate position, practise the art of originality, of doing each job a little better or by a better method than the rest of your fellow-workers. Become a leading subordinate and enjoy every opportunity of self-direction.

Nothing grows more rapidly than this habit of self-originated activity, and no bodily muscle shrinks more rapidly and fatally from disuse than this central feature of human leadership,

As a final word in urging you to prepare for leadership, let me advise that you never disobey or neglect the orders of your superior officers; also that you never allow yourself to be pushed or driven to your daily duties. Always of your own volition do a little more than is required of you and try to devise better methods of accomplishing any required tasks. Be assured that such habits will soon begin to promote you.

To be a doubly successful subordinate is the first step toward becoming a trebly successful boss.

Four-Square Manhood

"Show thyself a man."—I Kings 2:2

YOUR MANHOOD is your chief asset in life's great business, the most valuable and most indestructible of all your possessions, the richest dividend-payer of all your investments.

Stormproof, germproof, fireproof, panicproof, burglarproof; paying extra dividends in time of panic, growing more valuable when all other securities decline, unaffected by ill-health, exempt from all taxation, rated above par in every money market, making every owner a millionaire in heaven's unerring rating book, the one and only earthly possession which you can carry with you when at last you must leave all else behind—surely the young American who undervalues and lets his manhood deteriorate is a suicidal fool on the straight road to bankruptcy.

To value four-square manhood aright, to maintain it unsullied and unweakened, to nourish and foster its steady growth, to dedicate its purity and power to the advancement of human welfare, to root out and destroy whatever poisons its purity or checks its growth, this is at once your most urgent task, your weightiest obligation, your most inspiring opportunity.

Four-square manhood is not an accident, nor a lucky find, nor a fortunate inheritance. It is the complex product of the builder's art, representing the labor and self-denial of years. It is generally built, if built at all, during the formative years of youth and early maturity; and each of you is at once architect and builder of his own manhood.

Now, therefore, is the right time for you to memorize the right plans and specifications, set your own heart on fire with zeal for the great task, and strengthen your will power against every lust and appetite that tends to thwart your lofty purpose.

That your vision may be clearer and more definite and your endeavors more resolute and effective, I have come as an architect of long experience and wide observation to give you the plans and specifications of twentieth-century manhood, complete, symmetrical, well-rounded, Four-Square Manhood.

It has four essential elements, four rock-hewn cornerstones. The first of these is Courage, the backbone of manhood.

The shrinking and fearful, the hesitant and self-distrusting, the sneaking and cowardly—these may perhaps have some very lovable and commendable traits, but four-square manhood is not one of them.

Fear is the never-resting enemy of four-square manhood. It is not only in itself a torment, but it cripples our ambition, paralyzes our initiative, destroys all capacity for leadership, and is almost always a guarantee of ultimate failure.

This world in which we live and work is a battlefield, one's heart is a battlefield, living is an endless warfare; a thousand foes without and a thousand foes within are bent on defeating and enslaving us. A coward is unfitted for life's unending battlefield. He is destined to be forever the obedient tool or agent of others, never the leader or the conqueror, subject always to personal humiliation and defeat.

Like every attribute of the human personality, courage and strength of will are to be acquired and developed by constant and zealous practice. Timidity is both natural and universal in childhood. The growing man must get rid of it. Recognize all fears, little or big, as your enemies. Learn, therefore, to recognize them, to fight them, to overcome them.

To help make your thinking definite let me name three daily exercises in courage which will go far toward hammering your backbone into tempered steel.

(1) Do not shrink from hard jobs, disagreeable tasks, and weighty responsibilities. Attack them with the joy of battle in your eyes, and learn the joy of victory over a hated foe.

(2) Do not allow yourself to be overcome by superstitious fears, by unlucky numbers or signs or events, or by omens or ghosts or graveyards. There is no form of slavery so senseless and degrading.

(3) Rid yourself of the fear of unpopularity. We live in a crowd-filled and crowd-driven age. The very glory of moral manhood is to stand out from and above the crowd, like some cliff in a storm, defying the waves that beat helplessly against its immovable walls. The bane of young men and women massed in clubs or schools or factories is their chicken-livered cowardice in the face of their crowd's disapproval.

One rock-built defiance of "the gang" will set you far forward on the road to four-square manhood. Cultivate, therefore, every day, your will power, your willingness to attack anything and anybody that blocks your clear path of duty. Cultivate the habit of fearlessness, of independence, of scorning danger, of defying unpopularity.

With such a habit you will rid your life of a thousand unnecessary fears. You can work with serenity and effectiveness in a storm-tossed age or state; you can acquire even in youth the habit of victory, and win on life's tumultuous battlefield the iron cross of manhood.

Of the essentials of true manhood the second is Energy, the muscles of manhood.

Energy is as different from mere diligence or industry as the locomotive is from a patient obedient boxcar. The engine is the aristocrat of the road. It chooses the speed and the route. It always commands; the boxcars obey and follow.

All the workers on life's great four-track highway are of two types: the few engines, throbbing with energy, built to push and pull and lead, rich in the possession of surplus motive power, moving always under their own steam; and the vast multitudes of the merely diligent, those who follow, built after many varying designs but all according to freight-car blueprints, with no firebox, no steam chest, no motive power of their own.

Each of you in the formative period of youth is building himself into a freight car or a steam engine. If every day you stand on the track till somebody pulls or pushes you to your duties, you may be assured you are drifting into the freight-car class.

The secret of engine-building is cultivating the habit of energy, that means the habit of moving under your own steam. Let me assure you that the great busy world is hungry for men of the four-square engine type, and is eager to discover, promote, and reward them.

Attend, therefore, to your daily tasks, whatever they may be, attack your hated jobs, pay your debts, make your decisions—all under your self-originated motive power, without a word of command or reminder from anybody. Then, when your workshop days of youth are over, you will roll out on life's great highway under your own steam, a high-powered locomotive, built for life-long leadership, and sure of life-long success.

The third essential of all-round successful manhood is Love, the heart of manhood.

There are three distinct stages of man's growing civilization, whether we study him as an individual or as a tribe. The first is the child-era which worships strength. Its heroes are giants, pugilists, warriors, military leaders. The second is the intellectual era, which distinguishes early manhood. It worships knowledge and skill. Its heroes are those who win their laurels on the battlefields of thought, the eminent scientists, inventors, orators and statesmen and legislators. This worship of the intellectual marks the upper limit of merely material civilization.

But when our erring earthborn judgments are uplifted and enlightened by the spiritual and divine, we rise to a higher level and recognize that regal manhood reaches its culmination, not in physical strength nor intellectual pre-eminence, still less in riches or luxury or sensual gratification, but in love and sympathy and service.

Of all human attributes the power to love and to be loved is most nearly divine. Nothing so destroys human happiness, paralyzes human effort, and increases human misery as hatred and jealousy.

Fall in love with your work and your fellow workmen. Cultivate the habit of enthusiasm, of appreciation, of sympathy. As a generator of human happiness the heart far outranks the head. Be friendly and courteous to all, whatever their rank or station. Enrich your life with as many friendships as possible and your heart with the qualities of love and loyalty and unselfishness.

A cool head, an iron will, and a loving heart make an irresistible combination, not only on youth's playgrounds but all round the world. Remember that a loving heart is the throbbing center of a four-square manhood.

The fourth and highest of the basic elements of four-square manhood is Christian Consecration, the radiant crown of manhood.

Manhood which is of the earth, earthy, with no hold on things which are eternal and divine, no conscious union with God, no vision of the world to come—such manhood is hopelessly incomplete, dwarfed and one-sided, built, alas! upon the sand, unfitted to withstand the storms of life or stand serene and triumphant when death strikes his final blow.

If you would build your house of life four-square to all the winds that blow, if you would make sure that your courage will always fight on the right side, that your energy will always work for human betterment, that your love will always uplift and purify; if you would re-enforce the weakness of human nature with divine strength, then broaden your human vision till it sees two worlds instead of one. Add to earth's fleeting companionships a divine friendship that will outlast the grave. If you would set your feet, even here below among earth's fogs and shadows, upon that upward path that leads to the eternal sunshine; if you would begin, even here below where death and decay reign supreme, a life which will outlast the very stars themselves, then add to whatever else you may possess of manhood's attributes this crowning grace of spiritual consecration to the service of God.

Do not be misled by the cheap and shallow sophistry of the devil and his earthly allies into believing that a man's religion in the twentieth century is a thing of gloom and hardness, of narrowness and repression; that man finds a greater share of happiness in yielding to the brute desires of his animal nature, that modern science and modern criticism have shown religion to be mainly fables and superstition; that the best working motto of red-blooded manhood is "Let us eat and drink, for tomorrow we die."

All human history attests and all human experience proves that he who dedicates his life and its powers to the service of God and man is following the path, not only of the truest wisdom, but of the greatest happiness, and that the path of selfishness and sensuality is the sure road to misery, remorse, and endless ruin, whatever flowers may be strewn along its early stages.

Through life's varying experiences we are all on the way to our common resting-place in mother earth, but the paths that lead to it are infinitely varied and each must choose his own. Narrow, earth-centered lives, absorbed in the sensual, the base, the degrading, are following the valley road amid muck and mire and perpetual shade. For them, alas! there is no upward vision, no blue sky, no tonic mountain air.

But for every human pilgrim there is a possible road along the very mountain tops. It is a path made radiant by its very height, above mist and fog, above mire and undergrowth, with sunlit day and starlit night, where every earth-bound pilgrim may overlook his earthborn boundaries of time and space and claim immortal kinship with the eternal and divine.

Surely on this upward path, and on none other, shall earthly manhood, in conscious fellowship with God, find a career and destiny worthy of his divine origin and conscious immortality.

Three Fundamental Choices

THE HIGHEST of all man's faculties is his moral freedom, the power of deliberate choice between right and wrong. His most nearly divine inheritance is that inward monitor, the individual conscience, which holds him to an instinctive and eternal obligation to choose the right and reject the wrong, even when the wrong road is a bower of roses and the right a road of thorns. This is the royal prerogative, the divine compulsion, that lifts you and me so far above the plants and animals that surround us.

The dignity, the responsibility, and the danger of this moral freedom increase with every access of wealth, knowledge, liberty, leisure, or power. No gifts are so fatal to a community, a class, or an individual as increased liberty without a corresponding increase of self-control, increased wealth without increased wisdom, increased leisure without added moral culture, or newfound power without justice or sympathy or mercy.

This ever-increasing freedom and power are coming to our young people in this age of moral laxity and hysteric unrestraint. It will test their moral fiber to the uttermost. It is no wonder, then, that before such an audience I have chosen as a most practical and vital subject, "Three Fundamental Choices," and everyone of you must make all three.

FIRST, AN ORDERED OR AN AIMLESS LIFE

Building a character is as complex a task as constructing a modern business building. Suppose a builder were to purchase and pile around his chosen site stores of brick, cement, and stone, carloads of lumber, framing, ceiling, and flooring, and all the radiators, plumbing fixtures, hardware, and electrical materials needed; then assemble all his workmen, diggers, haulers, and carpenters, brick-layers, plasterers, and plumbers, pipe-fitters, and painters; and then order all to go to work at once, with no organization, no orderly sequence of operations, no single directing mind or purpose, no plans or blueprints or specifications.

You know the result—enforced idleness, constant friction, utter chaos, a constant process of tearing down and rebuilding. A house cannot grow. It must be first planned, then built.

So with your complex character, your important house-of-life, your priceless personality. Decide with wisdom and due deliberation what kind of character you wish to build. Make your character-ideals definite and complete. Prepare your plans and blueprints and specifications. Then resolutely build in accordance with them, encouraging this habit, repressing that, the whole an orderly, continuous, effective growth along carefully-chosen lines of character development.

In your daily work and play lead thus the ordered rather than the aimless life, the life of a regular daily program, fulfilling a fixed and definite purpose, a continuous progress toward a chosen goal, a life whose varied and manifold activities are all guided by a few, deep, all-powerful moral principles.

Compared with such a purposed life how weak and pitiful and ineffective is the aimless life, the life of impulse and emotion, the helpless victim of chance and circumstance. Such a life is a ship without a rudder, an auto with no steering gear, a traveler with no roads or maps.

If you wish to get anywhere or do anything in the world, if you wish to avoid weakness, fickleness, and certain failure, lead the ordered rather than the aimless life.

SECOND, A SELF-CONTROLLED OR A YIELDING LIFE

The first choice was a matter of character-building. This is more closely connected with your life progress, and I will draw my analogies from our systems of travel and transportation.

Youth is the character workshop and you are the builders. Building freight cars and trailers is easy and the materials are cheap and abundant. But to build yourself into a high-powered engine of steam and steel—that is a very different task. Yet it is certainly within reach of almost any one who is willing to make the effort necessary.

Cultivate, then, the everyday habit of moving under your own steam. Let every part of your day's program be carried out on your own initiative. Cultivate, always and everywhere, your own will power, your habit of *self*-direction, of performing every duty before any one reminds, or requests, or orders you.

Do not allow yourself to get into the habit of yielding to others. Be always ready to assume responsibility, to become the leader, to persuade others to take your point of view. Do not form the habit of "following the crowd." On a question of real honor, or duty, or principle never yield to anybody. Be stubborn as a rock.

Be sure to sweeten and consecrate an iron will with a warm, loving, sympathetic heart, and you will not only attain lofty ends but will have many devoted followers in a long retinue acclaiming your leadership.

THIRD, THE CENTRIFUGAL OR THE CENTRIPETAL LIFE

In every human society the selfish self-seeking life is natural, animal, instinctive, destructive. It always awakens opposition, jealousy, and strife. It always destroys love, peace, co-operation, harmony, and happiness, not only of the individual but of all who are associated with him. It is essentially opposed to religion and to civilization, both of which are based on mutual love and confidence.

The self-seeking life makes its own welfare and happiness its one supreme aim, yet owing to the nature of selfish desires and aims and the hatreds and jealousy awakened by them, such a self-centered life is never a happy one. It always generates unhappiness within and hatreds and opposition without.

Shun, therefore, as you would some dangerous disease, the symptoms and habits of the self-seeking life. These are jealousy, selfishness, envy, sarcasm, habitual criticism of others, disloyalty to friends, scorn and contempt of inferiors, rebellion against lawful authority, self-pity, self-conceit, self-praise—these are all poisonous weeds in your garden of life. Root them out whenever and wherever they appear above ground.

Compared with these baleful symptoms of the self-seeking life is the life that loves and serves, thus bringing the sunshine and harmonies of heaven down to earth.

Love is the sweetest, the mightiest, the most contagious thing in the world. "It blesseth him that gives and him that takes." Its very exercise is itself a source of happiness. Of all human faculties the power to love and to be loved is most nearly divine.

Our civilization reaches its culmination not in wealth, or power, or intellectual pre-eminence, but in mutual love, mutual sympathy, mutual service.

Would you find the golden passkey that unlocks all the doors to human happiness, to friendship, to leadership, to popularity and influence, to physical and mental health, to success, promotion, remuneration? Then cultivate now and always the faculty and habit of unselfish love and sympathy and service.

> For the soul that gives is the soul that lives,
> And bearing another's load
> Doth lighten your own and sweeten the task
> And brighten the homeward road.

The Christian Home and Its Enemies

THIS PERIOD of the twentieth century is one of rampart militarism all around the globe, of overturned governments, bankrupt nations, and paralyzed business at home and abroad. In our hitherto democratic Republic we find an era of universal conscription, governmental despotism, appalling annual deficits, and war-captured industries.

And so those who have planned this meeting have selected as the focus of our thoughts today and of our efforts as Christians in this momentous period this most appealing subject: "The Christian Home and its Enemies."

We are now in the midst of an era of world-wide warfare and world-wide transformation. The mightiest military despotisms of Europe and Asia are being torn to pieces by the peace-loving but now war-waging democracies of the United Nations of the whole world.

Old traditions, standards, modes of government, and national boundaries have been cast remorselessly into the melting pot. The next generation will see them slowly recrystallizing into the New World of Tomorrow; a new, and we trust a wiser and happier era of Christian civilization than our war-torn world has ever known in its past history.

As the luminous framework of our discussion let me impress upon every mind and heart a half-dozen important facts which bear witness to the supreme importance of the American home.

This is the first of these basic truths: That the children

of a self-governing republic like ours are by far its most valuable asset and its chief source of undeveloped riches and power.

The second is even more practical and compelling: That the right training of these future citizens constitutes the supreme task of a Christian democracy like ours.

This is the third truth centering our thoughts upon the homes and home-circles of our Republic: That a future citizen's habits and character, moral, social, and civic, are largely formed during the first six or seven years of his home life before his school training begins.

And these three impelling truths may all be gathered into a single awe-inspiring statement, which is this: The American homes of today are the *makers* and *builders* of the American civilization of tomorrow.

That our discussion may awaken constructive activity rather than any form or degree of discouragement, let me divide our review into three sections: First, some encouraging improvements in American home life which we may rejoice over and help onward; second, some recent modifications in American home life which every worker should recognize and to which he should adapt his efforts; and, third, some virulent enemies of the American home which should set on fire the fighting spirit of every true American.

Here are a few of the many improvements brought about in very recent years which we can all rejoice in:

We are today conquering and weeding out many home diseases, and the American homes of today know far more of practical hygiene and enjoy far better health than the homes of yesterday. How vividly do I remember the homes of my childhood and early manhood bereaved so often by typhoid fever, yellow fever, appendicitis, pneumonia, and many other diseases now so rarely fatal that their very names are unknown to the average family. We can today most heartily rejoice and thank God for the better health and the far longer life of the average American of today.

Another unspeakable improvement is the removal of the utter loneliness and isolation of all the country homes of yesterday, when country roads were often impassable all winter, country mail delivery unheard of, and not a single library or reading room in reach of country families.

Today with autos and good roads and buses everywhere, with Boy Scouts and Girl Scouts organized under inspiring leadership everywhere, with our traveling libraries and town libraries open to everybody, with public playgrounds and swimming pools open to all, with music clubs and camping parties and movie theaters in reach of everybody, with almost every church providing social life and recreation to its members, we can hardly imagine the winter loneliness of country children two generations ago.

And last, but by no means least, there are far better day schools and Sunday Schools everywhere to supplement and re-enforce the home-training of our young people.

Let us now mention three important modifications of American home life brought about by our rapidly changing civilization.

The first is the important change in the housing of the home circles of today. Two generations ago nearly every American family had its own house on its own lot, with front yard, backyard, and garden. Today thousands of our growing families are housed in small apartments in large apartment houses with no yards or gardens and no playgrounds except the city streets.

The second is the steady decline in the parental authority of yesterday, the growing independence of all young people of America of both sexes and all ages.

The third is the logical result of the first two: It is the steady growth of the away-from-home life of our young people.

The child of today leaves home for almost all of his daily amusement, recreation, and social life. The family fireside was once the home center, with the family table and very frequently the family altar keeping it close company. Today our young people sleep and take their meals at home but live and play elsewhere.

Let us now consider the enemies of the American Home and pledge undying enmity and wage unceasing warfare against them. I will mention seven of these venomous enemies, every one of them summoning us to earnest prayer for divine help, to active non-partisan citizenship, and to wholehearted, militant Christianity.

The first is our nation-wide moral breakdown, our nation-wide epidemic of theft and robbery and homicide, our loss of moral indignation against crime and criminals, our hysteric sympathy with law-breakers against law officers, our habit of setting prisoners free by a governor's pardoning power.

The second is our characteristic American dislike of any kind of law-restraint, our instinctive opposition to any kind of law, any kind of interference with our cherished personal liberty to do as we please. Of all civilized Christian nations America is the leader in the habit of lawbreaking.

The third is the new freedom for womanhood and girlhood. The old social rules and strict restraints have all broken down, and against this personal liberty our American girls have not yet developed the habit of stern self-control.

A fourth is the almost incredible omission of regular moral training in our tax-supported public schools of every grade from the graded schools to the state universities.

A fifth is the manifold opportunities for vagrancy, immorality, and easy lawbreaking furnished by our present-day abundance of good roads and swift autos.

A sixth is the increasing habit of selling and drinking

alcohol, the deadliest enemy in human history to purity, self-control, and right conduct.

The seventh, and the last which I will mention, is the number and cheapness of immoral movies attracting millions of young people in thousands of movie-theaters every hour of every day seven days in the week. The fact that the organized effort of millions of Christians has banished the utter vileness of the worst movies is a matter of sincere congratulation, but the danger is everywhere present and demands our ceaseless vigilance.

We Christians pray every day, "Thy kingdom come. Thy will be done *on earth*," here in our own city and state and nation, "as it is done in heaven itself." These seven enemies and their destructive attacks are calling every true-hearted American to the moral battlefield that our blessed boys and girls, as they grow towards maturity, may breathe a safer, purer, more invigorating air, freer from poisonous gases and moral disease germs than the air they breathe today.

Let us from this gathering go forth to devote ourselves more energetically than ever to the moral hygiene of our great nation. As our skilled physicians are conquering one physical disease after another, let us conquer these contagious moral diseases that the American civilization of tomorrow may be purer, more Christian, more exhilarating to our higher nature, than ever before in our history.

The Expanding Life

Two worlds of equal extent and sublimity lie open to every inquiring mind: the universe of matter without, with its millions of revolving worlds on their long road to death; and within, the universe of mind, no less sublime and infinite, with its spark of divine fire imprisoned in a tabernacle of clay, its fathomless depths of thought and feeling and volition, its unimaginable heights of love and sacrifice and aspiration.

My subject is "The Expanding Life," the life history, not of a shriveling, decaying, mortal world, but of a living, growing, immortal soul. I would make clear to your vision that infinite upward path by which the immortal spirit of man, rising steadily above pettiness and baseness, shaking itself free from ignorance and prejudice and narrowness, begins even here below a career of infinite growth and limitless development that shall outshine and outlast the very stars themselves.

The expanding life—its meaning, its inherent difficulty, its threefold process, its glorious rewards.

The expanding life is of course the growing life, marked by ever-widening knowledge, ever-multiplying interests, ever-deepening feeling, ever-broadening appreciation, ever-rising hope and aspiration. The ability to live such a life is at once the proof and the measure of man's greatness. No lesser ambition is worthy of his powers. To climb this uphill road is his privilege, his duty, his glory.

Let me remind you, however, that it takes time and courage and constant effort to lead the expanding life. The keynote of our twentieth-century civilization is organization. Its watchword is efficiency. Its aim is to make each individual a specialist in his own narrow line—and then chain him forever to the one task he has learned to do best. Unless this narrowing tendency is consciously and energetically resisted, every earnest and conscientious worker finds himself becoming more and more the contented bondslave of monotonous routine.

The business man whose outside interests have shriveled and fallen off till his petty office has become his whole world; the teachers whose early visions have faded into a dreary routine of lessons and grades and examination papers; the zealous wife and mother whose field of vision grows more and more limited till at last her whole horizon is bounded, north, south, west, and east, by the nursery, the dining-room, the kitchen, and the parlor; the social parasite to whom life has become but an endless round of shallow amusements; the laborer who knows nothing beyond daily toil, daily food, daily sleep; the farmer who never lifts his dead mind above the dead soil he tills—all these, and countless others like them, narrowing and shriveling as their ignoble lives creep by, bear pathetic testimony to the all-pervading pressure which we must resist and overcome if we would lead the expanding life.

How can we avoid a like fate? How can we achieve growth and expansion against this never-ceasing pressure? What are the methods and processes of the expanding life? As all growth is one, let us learn our lesson from the vegetable world. In what way have the life forces of a forest monarch lifted it against the never-resting pull of gravity to its present stature and eminence?

First, it grows in *Breadth,* multiplying its branches and thrusting them ever outward in search of more abundant air and sunshine.

Second, it grows in *Depth,* multiplying its roots and thrusting them deeper into the earth to anchor its growing bulk against wind and storm.

Third, it grows ever in *Height,* lifting its green crown

further from the earth in which its roots are set, nearer to the blue sky that calls it overhead.

So must *we* grow if we would lead the expanding life.

Grow, first of all, in Breadth. The bane of our petty routine lives is their tendency toward narrowness, provincialism, one-sidedness, hopeless partisanship under the guise of loyalty, hopeless bigotry under the sacred name of religious zeal, hopeless slavery to names, traditions, and shibboleths that have long since lost their meaning and vitality.

Grow in Breadth of Knowledge, feeding ever on new facts, digesting new problems, gaining new points of view, traversing new fields of human thought, human effort, human experience. If you are a specialist, be a broad man sharpened to your special edge. As the non-cutting mass of the axehead gives momentum and effectiveness to its cutting edge, so will general knowledge and wide experience add driving power to the thin edge of your specialty. Keep your mind, therefore, ever open, alive, hungry, growing.

Grow also in Breadth of Interests. Life is not measured by the calendar but by the multiplicity of its interests, the richness and variety of its experiences. A life of dull, narrow, monotonous routine, made up of daily toil, daily food, daily sleep—such a life has only one dimension. It is mere existence. The true content of real life is not a mere line. It is an area, its length multiplied by its breadth. If, therefore, the breadth of your life is zero, though your barren years may number fourscore, the product of the two, the length multiplied by the breadth, the real measure of your life, is by all the laws of life and of mathematics infinitely near to zero. Such a life is a starveling streamlet trickling over a stony bed. Let yours be a rolling river full to the brim.

But man is not made to live alone. With ever-expanding knowledge and multiplying interests let us grow also in Breadth of Sympathy.

If a narrow mind is a misfortune, a narrow heart is a tragedy. Love, sympathy, appreciation, unselfish service to others—these lighten the universal burden, oil the bearings of life's jarring machinery, lift the clouds that overhang every pathway, and waken in human hearts and homes the harmonies of heaven itself.

But the tree that grows in breadth alone without developing its root system ensures its own destruction in time of storm. The second essential element of the expanding life is increasing Depth.

The widespread blight of modern life is its petty, restless, hysteric shallowness; shallow knowledge that fails in time of need, shallow thinking that follows the crowd and applauds the demagogue, shallow love that dies on the very altar of home, shallow purposes abandoned at the first blow from an antagonist, shallow principles uprooted in time of storm.

Our age is an age of stress and strain, of world-wide warfare, revolt, and reconstruction; a very whirlwind of swift-crowding revolutions, social, political, economic, raging over our heads. Surely in such a stormy era breadth without depth is fatal. Let every tree of life develop a strong taproot. Let every house of life be built on the underlying rock. Let every human character exert itself to develop deep-rootedness, stability, fixed principles which no storm can shake.

The third dimension of the expanding life is Height. By the innermost law of its being, as the fulfilment of its life's fixed purpose, the growing tree is forever lifting its green crown further from the muck and mire of earth, nearer to the stainless blue of the eternal heavens. So must we climb ever upward if we would lead the expanding life.

Such is the meaning, such the difficulty, such the threefold process of the expanding life. May I exhibit, in conclusion, some of the radiant fruits that grow on such a tree, some of the benefits that reward its resolute purpose and high endeavor?

To the family, the community, the church, the state, the nation, such a life is a perennial source of help and inspiration, enriching itself continually and as continually dedicating its growing treasures to the common good. All the blessings of democracy at its best, efficient schools and consecrated churches, good roads and happy homes, social justice and industrial harmony, business honesty and cooperative efficiency–all follow fast where expanding lives like these set the pace and lead the way.

To the individual himself, and I am speaking to individuals, each with his own life to lead, five golden fruits hang, shining and resplendent, on such a tree of life.

The first is Wisdom and Sanity. The one-ideaed specialist, the bondslave of monotonous routine, the man who hardens and shrivels as the benumbing years creep by, carries even to gray hairs the crudeness and inexperience of youth. He must bear all the manifold ills of age without the ripeness and maturity which are at once its crown and compensation. He who leads the expanding life is always abreast of the age. He alone can see life sane and see it whole. He alone, through increasing knowledge and varied experience, can attain the broad judgment and ripened wisdom of age, while still in possession of the vigor and vitality of youth.

The second fruit of the expanding life is the distinctively American trait of Resourcefulness, the ability to light on one's feet in every emergency, to utilize unexpected opportunities, to win success in new fields of effort, to follow one's star wherever it may lead.

The third priceless result of the expanding life is perennial Freshness and Elasticity. Exposed to the unvarying monotony of unvarying routine, the human spirit, like live rubber under a heavy weight, becomes dead, brittle, inelastic. Would you keep yourself live, elastic, resilient? Then vary the daily pressure. Would you avoid mental stagnation and atrophied faculties? Then keep adding to your knowledge and multiplying your interests. Would you cheat the benumbing years and find for yourself the fountain of perpetual youth? Then climb out of the rut and lead the expanding life.

A fourth result of this threefold growth is Richness of

Life. A life without growth or variety, given over to monotony, satisfied with routine, is a drought-stricken streamlet trickling over a stony bed. Compared with such a poverty-stricken existence he who leads the expanding life is a millionaire in the things that count, and no thief or sharper can rob him of such wealth.

Rich in the treasures of human thought, human love, and human experience, his soul vibrating to a thousand chords, he can never be bored or solitary or lonely. His life is like a rolling river, full itself to the brim and enriching every plain through which it moves.

Such ripened wisdom and quick resourcefulness, such perennial youth and elastic resilence—these bring us to the last of these fruits of the expanding life—they give us a Dignity and Inspiration which the petty, the narrow, the shallow never know. He who lives like a vegetable and works like a machine has, indeed, sold his regal inheritance for a mess of pottage.

If there is an infinite Mind of whose vast plans our feebler intellects can catch inspiring glimpses, an over-ruling Purpose, which guides a billion stars in their fiery orbits, yet stoops to take a stumbling child of earth by the hand, a divine love which has transformed human life and been the inspiration of heroic souls in every age—if such divine companionship, such transfiguring love, such freedom from the bondage of the finite and transient *is* possible to man—then surely on this upward road and none other shall human life find a dignity and a destiny worthy of its divine origin and conscious immortality.

> Build thee more stately mansions, O my soul,
>   As the swift seasons roll!
>   Leave thy low-vaulted past!
> Let each new temple, nobler than the last,
> Shut thee from heaven with a dome more vast,
>   Till thou at length art free,
> Leaving thine outgrown shell by life's unresting sea!

III

Science and Its Influence

The Culture Afforded by Scientific Study

ALL HUMAN activity, whether of body or of mind, has two aspects and may be examined from two points of view: the inner, subjective effect on the mind or body thus exercising itself, and the outward, visible, objective result, which is generally the sole purpose of the action and the only effect noticed by the world at large.

Many forms of training, both mental and physical, have only the first end in view. The gymnast, for example, climbs the ladder or vaults the bar, not to get nearer the ceiling or over an obstacle, but to render his body more supple and powerful. The fireman, on the other hand, climbs ladders that he may rescue those in peril, and the pedestrian vaults over a fence that he may continue on his journey.

So all departments of study and intellectual endeavor may roughly be divided into two classes: those whose chief end is this reactive, subjective effect, the training and invigoration of the mind pursuing them, and the second great class sometimes scornfully called "The Bread-and-Butter Sciences."

Logic, metaphysics, the ancient languages, and pure mathematics are generally considered typical examples of the first, and have long been regarded by the majority of scholars as having pre-eminent cultural value. Those whose training has been confined to these departments often speak slightingly of the culture afforded by botany, physics, chemistry, or geology. They are inclined to class these studies with typewriting, telegraphy, and bookkeeping: excellent means of making a living, indispensable to our modern material civilization but devoid of spiritual power, commercial and practical to the core, cold and hard as the machinery which science has invented, pitiless and inexorable as the laws of nature which she has discovered, and incapable of affording a high type of genuine liberal culture even to their most ardent and single-minded devotees.

The purpose of my present address is the defense of scientific training as a means of culture. I am not here to discuss the obvious value of scientific study, or to call over the long roll of its magnificent achievements. They constitute the chief distinction of our age. Science is rapidly and continuously transforming our human civilization. It cleanses the slums of our crowded cities, sentinels our shores against the dreaded invasion of the pestilence, and by its surgery and medical skill drives back the destroying angel from a million homes. It lays its shining rails and strings its tiny wires through the blood-stained depths of a tropical forest, and sweet peace and happy homes and heaven-born religion take the place of lust and murder. It drives its marvelous tunnels through the granite heart of a mountain range, and nations, long separated and hostile, "like kindred drops" are "mingled into one."

It touches with its magic wand the rainless deserts of Egypt, of India, of Colorado, and the long-barren sands are like the garden planted eastward in Eden. Under trackless wastes of world-wide oceans science buries its wonder-working cables, and distant islands, long exiled from the life and sympathy and progress of humanity, come into their heritage once more and take their place at the family fireside of the nations. Through the airplane and the radio and the moving picture it is abolishing all boundaries and compressing our whole world into a single complex neighborhood.

The discoveries of science are at once the dominant note in modern history, the foundation stones of modern civilization, and the greatest impelling force in the world's progress today.

And the chief miracle of it all to me is the fact that, instead of reaching the limits of scientific research or exhausting the resources of nature, these wonder-working discoveries succeed one another faster and faster, till every-day realities surpass the dreams of yesterday. We are surfeited with marvels; the very sense of wonder is dulled; and we watch the magnificent panorama with a sort of stupefaction. The very air the scientist of today breathes is full of intellectual intoxication. He feels like some ardent mariner on the prow of a giant steamer rushing ever through strange untraveled waters and seeing new worlds rising every day out of the blue horizon.

But from this fascinating yet oft-told story of the practical triumphs of modern science, I turn to set before you the cultural value of such studies, their reactive effect on the mind of the student, the *type of culture* which they furnish our modern civilization.

Of what I conceive to be the four dominant characteristics of scientific culture the first is undeviating Truthfulness, or, in the language of science, Accuracy.

First, such training teaches the value of accuracy. However long and complicated a calculation may be, and however carefully it may be performed, one error, wherever committed, vitiates the whole. A fraction of a grain too much of this ingredient, or too little of that, vitiates the whole. The very genius of modern science is quantitative, and the laboratory brings to every faithful student an almost awe-inspiring realization of the value of accuracy. This is a lesson the majority of our race never learn.

Second, and more important still, is the fact that such training leads to habits of accuracy. These habits are:

(1) Accuracy of Sense-Perception and Observation. The experimenter must see just what happens, no more, no less. He cannot, according to common custom, mix his inferences with his observations, or the next series of experiments will plunge him into hopeless contradictions. The very basis of all the experimental sciences is accuracy of eye, ear, touch, and measurement. In no other departments of study are the senses trained to such keen discrimination.

(2) Accuracy of Measurement and Calculation. An error of a thousandth of an inch in linear measurement, or a thousandth of a grain in ascertaining weight, may vitiate a whole train of experiments. The scientific investigator learns to measure and weigh and calculate to the highest limits of accuracy which his instruments allow.

(3) Accuracy in Statement and Description. The aim of a scientific writer is to present in words the thing as it is. The ideal language of science is clear and transparent as a mountain stream. Every technical term has its precise meaning. There are no attempts at coloring or embellishment, none of the arts of the rhetorician, no profusion of adjectives, no merely decorative effects. A scientific paper is generally a model of clear expression, and you look in vain for vagueness, ambiguity, or obscurity. The value of such habits of expression is inestimable.

The second result of scientific training is Logical Habits of Thought. Let us examine this feature of scientific culture more in detail.

First, its extended drill in pure and applied mathematics is a thorough drill in pure and applied logic. Even the most ardent metaphysicians concede the pre-eminence of mathematical training in conferring logical and analytical power upon the minds nourished by its strong meat. Rigid, inexorable logic is the dominant note in all mathematics. The most important departments of science, such as physics, chemistry, engineering, and astronomy, are based on mathematics, and those pursuing these studies live in an atmosphere of mathematical reasoning. The mind of the ideal scientist thus becomes a very engine of clear, cold, remorseless logic. No such training can possibly be found in the study of civics, history, rhetoric, or the languages.

In the second place the chief aim of all experimental science is to trace the relation of cause and effect between apparently unrelated phenomena, and this relationship is the basis of most of our reasoning. I believe that two-thirds of all the fallacies that mislead the individual or the world at large have their origin in the misapprehension of this relationship. The untrained mind continually mistakes mere sequence or mere coincidence for the true cause-and-effect relation. Its motto is *"Post hoc, ergo propter hoc."*

For example, two generations ago the price of silver was very low. So, at the same time, was the price of wheat and cotton. The wheat planters of the West considered one cause, the other effect, and declared that wheat would never rise in price till silver was remonetized. One year later wheat reached the highest price in twenty years, while silver continued to sink. The cotton planters of the South sang the same tune, declaring that six-cent cotton would never rise till silver was remonetized. Not long thereafter Congress gave silver a death blow by putting the country on a gold basis; whereupon cotton, *mirabile dictu,* rose to ten cents a pound.

Some years ago a highly-educated man, not in science, however, proved to me, as he thought, with overwhelming logic that the phases of the moon had a powerful effect on bodily health and disease. This is his Socratic argument, verbatim: "Do you not admit that the moon powerfully affects the great liquid oceans of the world, disturbing equilibrium, and causing tides and tidal currents?" I answered "Yes." "Is not more than three-fourths of the human body liquid?" "Yes." "Does not the body's health depend on the condition and movements of these liquids?" "Yes." "If, then, the moon can violently disturb billions of tons of liquids in the ocean, can it not even more powerfully affect the condition and movements of the small amount in the human body?" And I answered "No"; for in spite of its syllogistic sound, the reasoning is fatally defective.

The scientist seeks to find the true causal relation between the moon and its tides, and asks whether this relation exists between it and the liquids in the human body. Mere coincidence in time cannot satisfy him. His whole lifework in the laboratory is to assign each effect to its true cause, in spite of coincidences which confuse and sequences which obscure this fundamental relationship.

In the third place, the study of science trains the mind to logical habits because every experimental investigation is a study in applied logic. Note the steps of such research: There is, first, the classification of heterogeneous phenomena; second, the discovery of a general law by induction; third, the theoretical deduction of new consequences from this law; and fourth, the experimental verification of this deduction.

Thus every laboratory is a school of applied logic, and the trained scientist is also a trained logician.

The third great gift which scientific training confers upon the mind is Freedom. Our language contains no loftier word nor one oftener dragged in the mire. The attainment of true freedom, with all which the word rightly connotes, is the high aim of statesman, philanthropist, and prophet. To strike the fetters from the slave, to open prison doors to the captive, to break the power of the oppressor and lead a nation into the clear air and sunshine of liberty—these are the deeds that echo round the world, and lift mere man to the place and power of demigods.

Yet as the immortal part of man excels his clay tabernacle, so is it a far nobler service to disenthral the imprisoned spirit and release men's minds from bondage than to release their imprisoned bodies.

Scientific culture gives Freedom from Narrowness and Provincialism. The scientist is the true cosmopolite or world-citizen. Scientific formulae are the only universal language, and scientific terms the only vocabulary common to all languages. All nations have contributed to the growth of scientific knowledge, and no student, however elementary, confines his study to the facts, theories, or writings furnished by his fellow countrymen. The laws and processes of nature take no cognizance of class distinctions, of national enmities, of racial prejudices, or of theological controversies. It is hardly possible to discover from the subject matter of a scientific treatise or from its mode of presentation in what country it was written, what creed its author held, or from what race he sprang. The first steps of scientific study thus lift its votary above narrow provincialism and introduce him to a true world-society.

The second chain broken by scientific culture is in giving Freedom from Stubbornness and Prejudice, one of the most subtle forms of intellectual slavery. No one, unacquainted with the history of scientific thought, can realize how tentatively the scientist holds his theories, or how incessantly his hypotheses are being recast. A textbook of physics, or chemistry, or geology, written twenty years ago seems almost ludicrous today, and every student feels that the hypotheses of today will be sifted, amplified, restated, or perhaps wholly rejected tomorrow. At any moment a single experiment may overthrow a theory of a century's standing, encircled by a halo of illustrious names and hitherto regarded as unassailable. Thus prejudice and mental stubbornness cannot coexist with the true scientific spirit, which holds all theories subject at all times to searching re-examination.

Science also gives Freedom from Bigotry and Intellectual Pride. No department of study brings one into such constant and humbling contact with the Unknown. The torch of science may double the radius of its effective illumination, but that only quadruples the area of encircling darkness that limits its feeble light on every side. In every investigation, from the simplest to the most complex, a few steps bring the experimenter to this inpenetrable wall of mystery, and he stands awed and humbled in the presence of the Unknown and apparently Unknowable.

He examines the laws of gravity, electricity, atoms, molecules, chemism, organic growth and decay, yet of the innermost nature of all these things he is utterly ignorant. Overwhelmed by the vastness of the Unknown, standing face to face with the mysteries of nature, the true scientist must in the end repeat the despairing cry of Newton, who, after reaching the summit of scientific knowledge and making his name immortal by his marvelous researches, declared, "I am but a child, playing with a few gaily-colored pebbles on the shore, while the great ocean of truth lies undiscovered before me."

Scientific training also gives its votaries Freedom from the Impositions of Modern Quackery.

Those who know nothing of the laws and processes of nature fall an easy prey to quacks and impostors. Perfectionism in the realm of religion, a score of frauds in the realm of medicine, electric shoe soles, hair brushes, and belts, electropoises, insulating bed castors, and the like, in the presence of whose unspeakable silliness and self-stultifying idealism a true scientist knows not whether to laugh or cry; divine healing and miracle working by long-haired peripatetics; all these and a score of other contagious fads and rank impostures find their followers among those who lack scientific training. Among their deluded victims are thousands of men and women of high moral character, undoubted piety, good intentions, charitable impulses, and literary culture, but none trained to scientific research. Vaccinate the general public with scientific training and these epidemics will become a thing of the past.

The last and most degrading form of slavery from which science releases the mind and soul of man is the Bondage of Superstition. From the African savage who cowers in terror before his fetish, and our own Negro who sees headless ghosts in the dark, to the Johns Hopkins Ph.D. whom I once saw refuse to take his place at a dining because there were thirteen in the circle, superstition holds its million slaves in blind bondage to unreasoning fear.

Between "unlucky" numbers and occurrences and the dire consequences that are believed to follow them the scientist looks for true causal connection, and finding none rejects them *in toto*. Hence, as a class, scientifically trained minds are free from these widespread superstitions. I have, therefore, no hesitation in saying that the release of the general public from this form of slavery will be in direct proportion to the general diffusion of scientific habits of thought.

We have seen that scientific training imparts to the mind Accuracy, Logical Habits, and Freedom. Its fourth, last, and greatest gift is hardest to name or define. For lack of a better word I will call it Inspiration.

A scholar may write volumes on Greek prepositions, or English synonyms, or Latin syntax, yet never once find his whole being thrilled with a sense of sublimity; never once see before him the blaze of insufferable glory, and hear the Voice saying: "Put off thy shoes from off thy feet, for the place whereon thou standest is holy ground." These visions come not in the library, but on Mount Horeb, where the soul is alone with nature and its God.

In the study of the material universe we learn something of the vastness of time and space. We are lifted above the littleness and inevitable debasement of our petty human lives by the grandeur of nature, by her eternal calm and infinite patience, by the wide sweep of her changeless laws. Here there is no sordid greed nor petty striving, no neighborhood slanders nor malice cloaked in honeyed words, no silly social fads, no yellow journals nor howling mobs, no filth or mire of "practical politics." How base and mean and unworthy do these things appear, how the din and clamor of our noisy world die into reverent silence when they are brought face to face with the hoary antiquities of nature and of the material universe, which is the concrete thought of God.

Such are some of the fruits of scientific study, such are the visions vouchsafed by science to the reverent minds that enter her mystic portals; and, believe me, it is worth a great deal in this little life of ours to catch ever and anon, above its petty, clamorous noises, the voices of the Infinite and Eternal, calling to our souls from the depths of time and space, and on the dusty, contracted bypaths of our daily lives

> To feel the jar of unseen waves,
> And hear the thunder of an unknown Sea,
> Breaking along an unimagined shore!

Applied Science in the Civilization of Tomorrow

THERE ARE two interacting elements in all human civilization, the human and the natural, since every human purpose and activity is determined or modified by man's natural environment.

A discussion of the human element would include the problems and activities of business and politics and government, of law observance and crime repression, of all international problems and difficulties, and of our present era of world-wide warfare.

Our flashlight picture of today will omit this complex and important segment of our civilization. We will try to give a realizing glimpse of what the natural environment will soon contribute to human comfort and welfare. Man's natural environment is the marvelous complex of nature's laws and forces which surround him from his birth and so effectively limit or advance his every activity.

From the very beginning of human activity, man's safety, happiness, and welfare have been measured by his conquest and utilization of nature's laws and forces, and his civilization from this point of view might be divided into three great divisions.

The first might be called the Muscular Labor Period, lasting from the beginning of the human race till about the time of our American Revolution, which made us an independent nation.

The second might be called by several descriptive names, but we will call it the Fuel-Power Age, when man discovered that by burning fuel he could create almost unlimited power. It might be called the Age of Steam and Steel or the Age of the Inventor and Engineer. It has been the most momentous and fast-moving of all ages of human history.

The third we are just beginning, probably the most wonder-working of all. I will call it the Synthetic Age. It might be more descriptively called the Age of Applied Chemistry, or the Age of Plastics and Alloys. To describe its present and future miracles would require a volume. I will therefore endeavor to give a mere glimpse of its various possibilities, which will soon make our present civilization seem as old-fashioned and out-of-date as stagecoaches and kerosene lamps are today. It will be marked by the rapid decline of the use of wood, brick, iron, and steel in housebuilding and manufacture, and especially in all moving vehicles of every type. Also by the diminishing use of cotton and wool in clothing materials, by the rapid decline of food production as the leading aim of farming, and possibly by the disuse of burning fuel for producing power. These standard materials will be everywhere replaced by the artificial products of synthetic chemistry and various alloys of the light metals, aluminum and magnesium.

The leading activities of merely human civilization may roughly be divided into four chief divisions, mining, manufacture, transportation, and intercommunication, the latter embracing all forms of education, social usages, and religion.

The Fuel-Power Age has just reached and passed its culmination, making the past two hundred years the most wonder-working of all human history. By utilizing the immense driving power of burning coal, gas, and oil, by using iron and steel without limit, by inventing and utilizing myriads of marvelous machines, the Fuel-Power Age has created a new world of which our grandfathers never even dreamed. The last half-century of this Power Age has so conquered space and time as to make of the whole world a single neighborhood and so revolutionized intercommunication as to make of this world-neighborhood a single whispering gallery.

By adding to this practical conquest of space and time the miracles of modern surgery and sanitation the Fuel-Power Age has in a single half-century practically doubled the average working period of every civilized human life. In this present era of power and speed, with these amazing aids to achievement, a single individual in his single lifetime can now equal the achievement of about a score of equally diligent human beings in any previous age.

And now, ending the first half of the twentieth century, we have already entered upon the next wonder-working era, the Age of Creative Chemistry, or, using a broader term, the Synthetic Age. Its swift transformation of our present civilization is soon to make the architecture, the machinery, and the vehicles of today as hopelessly out-of-date as the oxcart and hand loom of our ancestors. In the short space of a brief essay let me try to give you a fleeting glimpse of a few of the marvels of tomorrow.

First: The replacement of all the buildings, vehicles, and many kinds of utensils now made of natural wood, brick, stone, cement, iron, and steel by the new synthetic products of today and tomorrow, mainly the new plastics and alloys.

Second: The replacement of iron and 'steel in all kinds of uses and structures by the lighter metals, aluminum and magnesium, and their numerous alloys.

Third: The construction of roadways, bridges, bathrooms, walls, and countless other structures of lightgiving fluorescent materials.

Fourth: The air conditioning of homes, schools, churches,

theaters, and other buildings, giving rise to a vast new industry rivaling the auto-age industry of yesterday.

Fifth: The construction of all buildings of light plastics, re-enforced by the light alloys, a coming revolution in building which it would take a volume to describe fully. These new buildings will all be incombustible, will never decay, can be made to look new again by shower-spraying, and are all insulated against heat and cold.

Sixth: The realization of a new era of transportation, which has just begun. The new railways will be swift, noiseless, and all elevated, with each coach or freight car running separately and able, at any given station, to leave the rails and run on the highways delivering passengers and freight where desired. The very light, plastic autos will travel on non-collision roadways. The new private airplanes will everywhere be able to light on and depart from flat roofs or backyard landing places. All vehicles of every kind will run on noiseless air-filled tires.

Seventh: The management and utilization of all rivers from source to mouth, with irrigation and water power everywhere available, using cheap plastic pipes to convey water.

Eighth: The use of the new television for scores of purposes in school rooms, hotels, and homes, and on public newsboards, giving hourly news everywhere.

Ninth: The utilization of the new talking libraries, with thousands of cylinders, each containing a volume, taken out by citizens. Such a cylinder placed in a home or schoolroom or any gathering place will give, chapter by chapter, to the home-folks, the sick, the blind, the aged, the imprisoned, to everybody everywhere, the priceless contents of the public library.

Tenth: The filling of our hilly lands, and especially of all tropical lands, with carefully-nurtured forests for the never-filled demand for plastics and all sorts of wood products.

Eleventh: The possible discovery of how to burn up fuel, as our sun is doing all the time. Our burning by which we get most of our power is merely letting oxygen and coal unite, their clash giving the heat-power we use. If, like the sun, we could utterly consume our fuel, turning all its atomic energy into power, one handful of coal would heat and light a big skyscraper of New York for a whole year or transport a mighty steamer all round the world. This discovery would almost relieve the human race of all bodily labor and cheapen everything we build or manufacture or transport.

These mere glimpses at the future possibilities of our civilization, especially when we get rid of war and its fearful wastefulness, will give every reader at least a glimpse of what the future may hold for him or her.

The Recent Marvels of Inventive Genius

RADAR WAS THE invention that gave to the United Nations their victory over Germany, thus preserving what we call European civilization.

The radiant energy that issues from our blazing sun is a complex mixture of vibrations, traveling in straight lines in every direction at the speed of 186,000 miles a second. The human eye is fitted to recognize as light and color only about two octaves of the longer waves, being "blind" to all higher and lower vibrations.

These light rays can penetrate a vacuum, the atmosphere, most gases, and a few "transparent" solids. The absence of only these two octaves of light vibrations constitutes what we call total darkness.

The elaborate apparatus known as *radar* can both generate and receive short-wave radiation invisible to the eye and can "see" its own waves reflected from distant objects. These "echoes" of its radiated impulses appear on the radioscope as spots of varying intensity.

Unlike the longer light waves, these short ones can penetrate fog or cloud however dense, and as the radar generates its own waves the presence or absence of daylight makes no difference. However dark the night or dense the fog or clouds a radar on ship or plane can thus "see" a ship, plane, fort, or shore line and determine its exact direction and movement. By measuring the millionths of a second required for the return of its waves the attacking warship or warplane can also determine the exact distance of the attacked object and thus destroy it with shells or bombs, while the threatened enemy can see and know nothing of the attackers.

This was the discovery that conquered German bombers and submarines and finally won the Second World War in Europe. It also slowly conquered the vast ocean empire of Japan, although at great cost of American soldiers, planes, and ships, and we were just ready to invade the Japanese home islands when a second and far greater invention, the atomic bomb, brought Japan's sudden collapse.

A half-century ago chemistry regarded the atom as the ultimate indivisible unit of which all matter is constructed. Hence it was named from the two Greek words a-tom, which means "non-cuttable" or indivisible.

Led by the radium studies of Marie and Pierre Curie in 1898, who discovered that radium atoms explode spontaneously, the scientists of every civilized country began researches looking for some method of decomposing atoms and utilizing their immense whirlpool power.

During the First World War the German Kaiser kept several large laboratories busy on this problem that he might be freed from dependence on imported fuels for his war engines. Finally, in the '30s, giant electrical atom-smashers were invented by several physicists, especially in the United States.

During the Second World War England and America, aided by several German anti-Nazi scientists who had escaped from Germany, united their efforts and constructed vast laboratories in the United States because of its relative safety from spies and attack.

Whole cities were built to contain fifty to seventy-five thousand inhabitants, and the surrounding area was carefully guarded to keep them and all their operations a dead secret. Immense atom-smashing cyclotrons were built weighing hundreds of tons.

An atom is composed of a dense nucleus surrounded by whirling electrons. In all nature there are 92 different kinds of elemental substances each with its own distinctive atom. The simplest atom is that of hydrogen, which has one electron circling round its nucleus. The most complex is the uranium atom with 92 electrons whirling about its complex nucleus.

The small size of an atom is really inconceivable. The nucleus is about one trillionth of an inch in diameter, and the diameter of the circling electrons is one 250-millionth of an inch.

The dense nucleus is made up of particles called protons and neutrons, sometimes as many as two hundred of them. The distance of the whirling electrons from the nucleus is at least five thousand times the diameter of the nucleus.

The complex uranium nucleus consists of 92 positively charged protons, each one holding a spinning electron, and 140 neutrons which are electrically neutral. If in any way the uranium nucleus can be disrupted, part of the atom's mass is converted into heat-energy, and this causes an immediate explosion.

There are three kinds of uranium atoms, each containing 92 protons but differing in the number of neutrons in the nucleus. The atom containing 92 protons and 143 neutrons is called U-235, and can be disintegrated with tremendous released energy by shooting into its substance a slow-moving neutron. To do this demands vast machines and very expert knowledge known to a very few English-American specialists.

Sir James Jeans tells us that the energy derived from the annihilation of a single drop of water would give us 200 horsepower for a whole year. It now seems that triumphant chemistry will in the near future make power, light, and heat almost as cheap and universal as air and water are today.

The first atomic explosive was tested in the rugged mountain section of southern New Mexico at 5:30 A.M., July 16th, 1945. A steel tower a hundred feet high was erected, with a massive ball weighing about 150 pounds at its top. The wires to cause the dropping and explosion of the bomb were carried to a deep underground station six or eight miles distant, and the connections made at the above hour.

When the ball fell, a terrific explosion, with a glare many times brighter than the midday sun, threw a vast cloud of flaming fire several miles high with a roar that baffled description. Men five miles away were knocked down by the blast. The steel tower dissappeared, and a vast crater half a mile wide was torn in the ground, with the sand at its bottom fused by the heat.

On August 5th the first atomic bomb of the war was dropped on Hiroshima, a city with a normal population of 344,000. It practically destroyed two-thirds of the city, killing at least a hundred thousand of its inhabitants and wounding as many more. The second atomic bomb was dropped on Nagasaki three days later, completely destroying over half of the city's area. No words can describe the appalling completeness of the destruction. Great tongues of flame leaped miles high, and the fierceness of the heat reduced a square mile of the city to a mass of white and black ashes.

The Russian attack on August 8th at midnight on the whole north border of Manchukuo was hardly needed after this bombing to cause panic throughout Japan, and the war closed with its full unconditional surrender a few days later on August 10th.

The atomic bomb marks a new era in world history. It makes war race suicide, but converted to peaceful use may open a new era of power, comfort, leisure, and human welfare.

IV
The Present-Day Call of Religion

A Brief Talk on Religion

RELIGION, IN its most general terms, is a practical recognition of the existence and claims of God, of our duties and obligations to Him, and of our future accountability to Him for our actions.

There are three instinctive, necessary, and universal desires of the human race. These are physical hunger, that the individual may not die; sexual hunger, that the human race may not die; and spiritual hunger, worship, adoration, religion, that man's soul, his higher nature, may not die. Of these, the third alone distinguishes man from the beasts that perish and opens to him all the possibilities of a higher future life.

Religion is coeval and coextensive with mankind. The human heart in every age and clime and degree of civilization has always knelt in reverence before a Higher Power and prayed for its succor and companionship.

No savage tribe has ever been found so brutal and degraded, no age so far back in the night of time, as to be without its gods. Religion of some kind is an instinctive and universal attribute of the normal human being, not an accident nor a temporary phase of human civilization.

It is also necessary to the very existence of the human race. In their individual and social life the animals are protected from suicidal excesses by imperious and controlling instincts. To man alone has been given the divine yet infinitely perilous gifts of mentality and moral freedom. He alone can paralyze his higher nature and stimulate his lower by artificial means, till he becomes a fiend incarnate whose unrestrained orgies of lust and cruelty would soon extinguish the race but for the restraining influence of some kind of religion.

The religion of a nation is by far the most important factor in determining its stability, progress, prosperity, and power. All history, ancient and modern, proves that nations rise or fall, grow wealthy or poverty-stricken, law-abiding or criminal, prosperous or bankrupt, strong or weak, not according to their numbers, area, climate, soil fertility, or natural resources, but mainly according to the religious principles they adopt and practise.

The half-desert hills of Palestine, the foggy and barren moors of Scotland, the rocky hills of New England, the marshy sand-flats of Holland, have, through the marvelous influence of their religious ideals and of these alone, been the prolific nurses of all that makes human civilization great—liberty and justice and virtue and patriotism, art and literature and science and philosphy; while nations inhabiting island paradises and river plains crammed with fertility, and owning mines stored with inexhaustible treasures, which have yet lacked an uplifting faith, have disintegrated and decayed.

It is not our climate and resources that have lifted our section of North America so far above Mexico and Central America and Brazil and the Argentine, all equally blessed by nature, but the type of character and conduct produced by our religious ideals. With all its weaknesses and faults our country's religion is by far her most fruitful and valuable asset.

The system of ethics and brotherly kindness taught in the United States every Sunday to scores of thousands of congregations and scores of millions of children is the mightiest enginery for curbing human lust and greed and cruelty and advancing human happiness and welfare ever set in motion by any single nation in the world's history.

If its lofty principles of brotherly love were universally acted upon by our people, the happiness and harmony and prosperity of the United States would surpass all the records of human civilization.

Such is the importance of religion to a state. It is a perpetual stimulus to all that is highest and best in human nature. It makes its votaries honest and honorable in all business transactions, just and generous to all employees, faithful to every duty and obligation, prompt and liberal in relieving distress, chaste and faithful in all domestic relationships, free from cruelty, tyranny, and avarice, and striving ever, with divine help, to follow the Golden Rule.

No wonder that all over the United States our leading citizens in all the walks of life—editors and authors, statesmen and administrators, merchants and manufacturers, lawyers and doctors and engineers—are all almost without exception religious men, and with every passing year the exceptions are becoming fewer.

But it is upon the heart and life of the individual himself that genuine religion bestows its richest blessings. It lifts his sources of happiness above the accidents of birth, station, and circumstance, and above the misfortunes of sickness, poverty, and loneliness.

It gives courage in conflict, comfort in bereavement, strength in time of weakness, serenity amid misfortunes, and a steadfast anchor to the soul in time of storm. It rids us of our most appalling fear by making death itself a friend in disguise.

Surely for the nation, for the citizen, and above all for the individual himself, the right kind of religion is an inestimable asset, and to go through life without it an irreparable misfortune.

The Bible and Our Moral Standards

OVER FOUR hundred years ago, in 1545, in the midst of the savage cruelty and widespread anarchy of the Middle Ages, when the Bible and its heavenly message were kept concealed in an unknown tongue and the representatives of religion were condemning to death all who opposed or disbelieved their creed, our Holy Bible was first given to the people in printed form in a language they could all understand. This was due to the great German Christian, Martin Luther.

The eagerness with which the people of Germany welcomed and treasured and studied this heavenly message is witnessed by the fact that they took up 80 editions of the New Testament within two years and 337 editions of the whole Bible or parts of it before Luther's death twelve years later.

One year after Luther's Bible appeared, Tyndale had visited Luther and translated the New Testament into English. Like so many others who tried to give the Bible to the people, Tyndale paid for it with his life.

The central features of our religion are set forth in the Bible: the life-history of Christ and his mission, the teaching of Christ and His inspired apostles all centering on love, the fatherhood of a loving God, the brotherhood of all mankind, the glory of self-sacrifice for the good of others.

With this background let us now give a flashlight view of the five wonder-working results of this Biblical message and its ideals in the moral standards of our modern civilization, especially in those nations which were lifted to world-influence and world-leadership by their loyal acceptance of the Bible and its message.

The first practical result of this biblical message on our civilization which I will mention is what I might call the growing tenderheartedness of our modern civilization, our growing sensitiveness to the suffering of other people, our growing feeling of obligation to care for the helpless, the diseased, the insane, the orphaned and destitute, and all everywhere who are unable to care for themselves.

This tenderheartedness was practically unknown in world history until the Bible in the people's tongues began to circulate widely among the masses. Every Bible-reading land today is strewn with orphan asylums, free hospitals, homes for the aged, asylums for the imbecile and the insane, free hospitals for the injured, public nurses for the sick, children's homes for the orphaned, and a vast Red Cross organization to come to the help of whole communities anywhere in the world which may be stricken by pestilence or flood or famine.

Search all the blood-stained pages of non-Christian human history, and never till our blessed Bible gained free circulation and began to convince men of their essential brotherhood will you find even a trace of gentleness or sympathy or help on the part of the powerful toward the weak and helpless.

Nothing is to me more appalling than the universal reign of cruelty and the oppression of the weak in all non-Christian civilizations, and especially the fearful torture chambers maintained by those calling themselves Christian for every outsider who refused to accept their exact creed and acknowledge the miracle-working of their leaders.

Only a few generations ago there were thirty or forty crimes punishable by death in England, and helpless infants were maimed and horribly disfigured by professional beggars to excite sympathy and make their begging more profitable. In our own country the first law ever passed making cruelty to children short of death a crime punishable by law was in 1876, only a little over two generations ago.

Surely, in the growing tenderheartedness of our modern civilization, removing new forms of cruelty with every generation, the teachings of the Bible have borne rich fruit in advancing human brotherhood and tender-hearted sympathy toward the weak and suffering.

As a second result of the circulation of the Bible and the spread of its principles of human brotherhood let me now mention the steady diminution and final abolition of human slavery.

This devilish custom of buying and selling human beings, of enslaving war captives, conquered nations, and the helpless savages of undeveloped continents was the universal custom of the human race till the wide circulation of the Bible four centuries ago began to teach our reading nations the fatherhood of God and the brotherhood of all men of every race and clime. Only three-quarters of a century ago human slavery was regarded by our Southern people in the United States as the right solution of the labor problem.

It seems almost incredible to us of the present generation that any brute in human form could have been allowed to buy at the auction block immortal human beings of both sexes and hold them as long as they lived subject to his own tempers, lusts, and passions, as much his property as his dogs and horses.

The circulation of the Bible, the growing tenderheartedness of Bible-reading nations, and the total abolition of long-established human slavery are surely linked together as cause and effect.

The third wonder-working moral effect of the wide circulation of the Bible during the last four centuries is the spread of a moral doctrine never held in all human history by non-Christian nations. This is that it is the moral duty of what we call the upper classes to furnish the many blessings of education and right training to all of our young people however poor and friendless.

In no line of human action is the all-human brotherhood so emphasized in the New Testament by our Savior exerted so wisely as in those Bible-reading nations which today open the doors of education and achievement to all of a nation's children, however poor, totally disregarding the fact that the children of the poor always far outnumber the children of the rich or well-to-do.

Even the most careless student of modern history must soon discover that even among professing Christian nations that keep the Bible in an unknown tongue and among all heathen nations the helpless poor become beasts of burden with no hope of advancement.

This free education for all, whether rich or poor, thus enabling even poor boys with genius to become judges, governors, and presidents, is the very salvation of a self-governing democracy like ours from the despotic tyrannies that have so recently wrecked both civilization and human brotherhood in so many countries of Europe and Asia.

A fourth and very recent effect of the spread of the Biblical ideals of human brotherhood among Bible-reading nations is the marvelous spread of brotherhood organizations throughout the Bible-reading world, and especially in our own America.

America has been swept by a marvelous epidemic of fraternal organizations, millions of Americans coming together in loving groups in such warm friendship that all religious, political, partisan, and national differences have been forgotten in this new and cordial affiliation. Let me name a few of them:

Among the young Americans of both sexes in colleges and universities, fraternities and sororities, social clubs, dancing clubs, study clubs, with debating clubs and athletic organizations on every campus.

Among the older Americans, such luncheon clubs as the Rotary, the Kiwanis, the Civitan, the Lions, and the rest. Among business leaders, Chambers of Commerce, Exchange Clubs, and Business Clubs without number. Throughout every city, the Garden Clubs, the Parent-Teacher Associations, the Boy Scouts and Girl Scouts, the Y.M.C.A. and Y.W.C.A., the countless "circles" connected with our churches and Sunday Schools, the annual conventions of every separate class of professional men and women—all these, old and young, married and single, rich and poor, gathering in every kind of social meeting, regardless of religious creeds or denominations —surely never in human civilization has their been such an epidemic of Christian brotherhood as has swept Christianity during the last few generations.

I will mention but one more of these Bible-wrought changes in our moral standards and moral judgments. It is the growing determination of Bible Christians in almost every Bible-reading civilization to abolish the devilish method of settling international difficulties by human warfare.

Settling international antagonisms by the wholesale murder of one another is in accordance with the non-Biblical theory that in human affairs might makes right.

The growing influence of the Bible and its ideals of human brotherhood have during the past century united most of the Bible-reading nations in a great international League to abolish warfare as a means of settling international difficulties, substituting therefor a World Court.

As our final word, therefore, on the increasing influence of the Bible and its ideals of human brotherhood and human welfare, let every true-hearted American Christian use all his influence by tongue and pen to swing our great nation into the heartiest effort not only to abolish militarism at home but to make permanent and all-powerful the United Nations and the **World Court.**

Tested by Fire

DANIEL III—SHADRACH, MESHACH, AND ABEDNEGO

WE ARE all, by nature, hero-worshippers, every one of us cherishing in his inmost heart some ideal of character to which he yields instinctive homage. A man's own character is best revealed, not by what he *says*, but by what, down in his inmost heart, he most *admires*. Hence the objects of our hero-worship are as varied as our own characters, and the ideal of manhood or womanhood toward which one heart lifts itself in loving loyalty may excite the aversion or even the ridicule of another.

Yet in spite of all diversity of taste, training, and temperament, I venture to assert that no tribe, or race, or individual ever admired cowardice, or failed to make *courage* an essential attribute of ideal manhood. From the earliest ages men have deified the battle-hero, and every land is strewn with monuments to the physical courage, the brute fighting passion, which dares a conflict with overwhelming odds and laughs in the face of death. That rarer and loftier courage, the moral heroism that dares do right when the right is an object of scorn and the wrong is easy and popular and remunerative, the world is but slowly learning to recognize and estimate at its true value.

To bring before our minds and hearts a scene from the Word of God where both these forms of heroism are united and conspicuously displayed cannot but uplift and inspire us, for the mind grows by what it feeds on, and the contemplation of lofty deeds tends to awaken our contempt for those that are base and low.

Let us go back, then, twenty-three hundred years and join the throng that pours in and out of Babylon's hundred brazen gates. Nebuchadnezzar is at the height of his power and glory, and his mighty capital, Babylon, with its vast walls and fortifications, its hanging gardens and temple of the sun, on which two million workmen have spent their strength and skill, is the gateway and center of the world's commerce and the wonder of the nations.

The giant power of Assyria, their hated oppressor for centuries, has at last been broken; Phoenicia has submitted to Nebuchadnezzar's authority; the dominion of the Egyptians in Asia has been annihilated and their shattered armies driven back into Africa; the Israelites in their fair land have been unable to escape the king's displeasure or to withstand his power; and so Jerusalem is today a mournful heap of ruins. The foxes and jackals wander unmolested where a few years ago the golden temple of Solomon glittered in the tropic sunlight; and her people, carried captive to heathen Babylon, are hanging their harps on the willows that fringe the Euphrates and mourning for their lost home.

Bring before your eyes the scene which the finger of God has immortalized. The level plain of Dura, stretching away to the shore of the Euphrates; the swarming myriads in holiday attire from every province of a world-wide empire; the thousand royal musicians ready to shake the very earth with the sound of trumpet and harp and dulcimer and all kinds of music; the King himself with his glittering train of courtiers and tributary princes; and in the center of the vast concourse the great idol of gold, symbol of the king's power, towering a hundred feet above the plain. Hear the heralds as they cry aloud in the many languages of the empire, bidding all at the royal signal to fall down and worship the king's image or suffer a horrible death.

Now turn your eyes to those three Jewish exiles, Shadrach, Meshach, and Abednego, facing the supreme temptation of their lives! They are standing at the place where two roads meet and part, and the fateful decision cannot be postponed or evaded.

On one hand life lies fair and full of the richest promise before them, a life of honor and exalted station, of wealth and ease, of power and royal favor. Already they are the chosen counselors of the great king, almost his adopted sons, the chosen rulers of the central province of his vast empire. There is no pinnacle of earthly power they may not attain, no dream of human ambition too fair for them to cherish.

On the other hand lies a road, short, sharp, and terrible; for it leads straight into the mouth of the roaring fiery furnace. To choose it is to lose everything men hold dear—reputation, rank, wealth, power, and the favor of the great. To choose it is to suffer everything that men fear and dread—shame and humiliation, the hatred and contempt of former friends and allies, and the agonies of a frightful death.

And now, while the musicians are getting ready and the crowds are surging closer to the giant idol, it seems to me we can almost hear the voice of the arch-tempter whispering his devilish suggestions into their hearts already so sorely tried.

"Bow down like the rest, but make it a real act of true worship, praying to your own God. You will thus save your lives without being guilty of idol-worship. Remember that anything is lawful to save one's life.

"At the worst it is but a harmless concession to popular clamor. When one is in Babylon let him do as the Babylonians do. Every one knows that it is a mere form anyway. There is nothing intrinsically wicked in falling down at the king's command, if your hearts are not guilty of idol worship.

"Remember that the king is not only your benefactor but your foster father. He has raised you from poverty and captivity to high rank and great power. He has clothed, fed, and educated you at his own expense. It is base ingratitude not to obey his command and show at least an outward reverence for this golden pillar, the symbol of his power.

"Be careful lest in your stubborn folly you defeat the purposes of the very God you profess to serve. He has worked miracles for your preservation and other miracles to bring you to your present place of power and opportunity. He has evidently a great work for you to do for your oppressed fellow captives and your once mighty nation, now homeless and exiled.

"Who knows but he may be thus preparing you to lead the great king himself to a knowledge of the true God of Israel, and then, like a second Moses, to lead your people back once more to the land of their fathers. Think what your lives mean for the welfare of your nation and the furtherance of God's mighty plans, and do not throw them away in foolish stubbornness over a mere form.

"Think, too, of the agonies of such a death, with every nerve and joint and sinew roasting and crackling in those sheets of flame. Think of all these things and do not throw away such valuable lives, with all their future promise, for a trifle."

What was their answer to these suggestions of Satan? Do you admire courage? Listen to their dauntless words. "Be it known unto thee, O king, that we will not serve thy gods nor worship the golden image thou hast set up." There is no shilly-shallying in that brave speech; no "cannot," "must not," "would rather not"— No; "We *will* not serve *thy* gods." Is it physical courage you admire? That speech consigns them to the burning fiery furnace. Is it the highest type of moral courage you seek? Then remember that among those hostile thousands they stood friendless and alone. It is an easy thing to charge a battery and risk your life on the field of battle, amid the cheers of thousands, the thunder of cannon, and the inspiration of martial music, when the soldier knows that a grateful country will enshrine his name among her heroes, and if he falls will care tenderly for his wife and children.

Yes, that is easy. It is often mere hysterics under a nobler name. But to die a dog's death, as an ingrate and traitor, amid the contempt of former friends, that is heroism of a different type!

What was the hidden source of such sublime courage? Their sublime courage was born of their sublime faith. Among those hostile thousands they felt that "One, with God, is a majority." Calmly trusting in the God of their nation, whose right arm had so often brought deliverance to their fathers, they despised the pomp and glitter of a heathen court and the transient power of the monarch of Babylon. He might burn their bodies with fire and scatter their ashes to the winds of heaven, but their free souls were beyond the reach of his impotent rage. The valley of the shadow of death was sown with fire, but their feet did not falter. The Son of God was waiting for them in the midst of the flames.

To the eyes of the multitude those massive bars of glowing iron were the very gates of death; to the faith and courage that defied death, they became the blessed portals into the audience chamber of the Most High. As it was then, so has it been from the beginning; so will it be to "the last syllable of recorded time." This lofty courage born of faith has sustained the followers of God amid the horrors of the dungeon, the rack, the guillotine, and the stake. No Alpine heights have been too cold, no fiery furnace too hot, for Him to meet His followers. No medieval dungeon has ever been too deep and dark for the sunlight of His smile.

There is no need to rehearse the remainder of the story.

The faith of Shadrach, Meshach, and Abednego was the faith that always conquers; it knows no defeat. God vindicated their trust in Him; the king was astonished and humbled; the rank and wealth and power they were so willing to sacrifice on God's altar were doubled and restored to them; and their heroic act was recorded for all time by the finger of God Himself.

The giant walls of Babylon have long since been leveled with the plain; her hanging gardens, the wonder of the world, have disappeared; her palaces and temple of the sun, her wartowers and citadels, her hundred gates of brass, have long ago crumbled into dust, and antiquarians dispute as to her very site. But the memory of this act of loyalty to God has never died or crumbled to decay. The great king of that Babylonish empire is known to the world of today chiefly because of his connection with these heroes of faith, and today, wherever the Gospel has spread, in every land and clime, in every spoken and written language known to man, their story of faith and courage is still stirring the hearts of men.

And now, what lessons may *we* learn from this story of faith and courage? What great truths, applicable to every age, every land, every life, does it illustrate and enforce?

Among many it surely teaches this—that all times in our lives are not of equal interest and importance. No life runs with even steady flow. As the sunglass gathers a thousand rays into one dazzling white-hot focus, so into one brief moment may be crowded the weal or woe of our whole eternal future. One vital momentous decision may determine the future trend of all our activities, may open the gate of a life of usefulness and honor or fasten in our bosom the fangs of a never-dying remorse.

These are the times that try men's souls and determine their fate. Today the sailors are lounging on deck, singing snatches of careless jolly sea songs, playing jokes on one another, or fast asleep in the shade of the idly flapping mainsail; tomorrow, with set teeth and muscles strained to the utmost, they are battling with the elements. No careless slumber now, no idle songs, no happy laughter. Out on the heaving bowsprit, standing firm at the wheel, far aloft on the swaying crosstrees, every man is at his post, while the moments creep by like hours and the hours seem days of agonizing suspense.

What makes the difference? Ah! Yesterday there was a blue sea below, a blue sky above, and a fair wind behind. Today their frail craft is in the grasp of a tornado and every man on board looks death in the face.

So in the monotonous routine of our daily lives there comes, often suddenly and without warning, one of those critical moments when great interests are at stake and the long years tremble in the balance. No tempest's roar warns us when the immortal soul is in danger of shipwreck. We ourselves may never dream that the passing moment is so big with fate.

When the Spirit of God breathes an influence unfelt before over the heart, and the prodigal son looks toward his Father's home; when some great affliction, warning us of the transient nature of all earthly joy, bids us look elsewhere for our highest happiness; when some great opportunity is opened to us; when we form new ties, new friends, new associations; when we first step beyond the blessed circle of home-love and parental guidance and assume the responsibility of self-direction; and especially when some direct temptation assails the soul, and we are called, like Shadrach, Meshach, and Abednego, to choose between the Right and the Advantageous; when Satan raises some idol of gold on our plain of Jura and orders us to bow down or pay the penalty; when our evil nature, our awakened passions, our besetting sins, rise up in open rebellion against right, and purity, and God.

It may be in the darkness of the night, in the solitude of

our own room; it may be in the still deeper loneliness of one soul striving to do right amid a host of evil companions; there is no roar of cannon or rattle of musketry, no floating flags nor battle cheers nor burst of martial music—yet there, on the silent battlefield of the human heart, may be waged a sterner struggle than ever reddened the Pass of Thermopylae or thundered over the hills of Gettysburg: "Greater is he that overcometh his spirit than he that taketh a city."

In a world so full of aggressive evil these testing times of conflict and of peril come to anyone at any age; but I believe that more of them are crowded into the formative years of boyhood and girlhood than in any other part of our lives, at the very time when worldly and sinful pleasures are brightest and most alluring, when every temptation is seconded by the thoughtlessness and ardor of youth, when new habits are forming for good or evil, when popularity and the applause of men often seem the highest attainable good; at this time of change and conflict and transformation, removed, as so many of my hearers are, from the restraints of home and home associations, freed from the oversight of pastor and Sabbath School teacher, out of reach of a father's guiding hand and a mother's loving voice, and placed in a world of new associates, new traditions, and new standards of thought and action.

Take heed, then, I beseech you, for you may be standing in slippery places. Here in this very locality, where there is so much to elevate and inspire, souls as precious as yours have been led astray; hopes as fair as yours have been forever blighted; and intellects as well fitted as yours to bless the world have been rendered a curse to their possessors and to all within the circle of their influence. Homes as blest and dear as yours have been shrouded in gloom; and hearts as loving as those now gathered around your home firesides have been crushed and broken—because even in this place of high privilege and opportunity the hope and pride of the family circle has proved recreant to the sacred trust committed to his hands.

In this fair morning of life you stand, like Shadrach, Meshach, and Abednego, at the place where two roads meet. Two paths are stretching away beneath your feet, meeting now in these careless sunny hours of youth, but diverging further and further apart as the swift-fleeting years glide by. On one hand lies the upward road, leading through a life of usefulness and consecration to the very throne and presence of Almighty God. Up-hill? Yes! uphill all the way, but every step upward brings you to a wider horizon and a more tonic mountain air. Rough, hard, stony? Yes! all three, but up that rocky pathway the mightiest spirits of all the past have trod their way to glory.

On the other side lies the downward road, strewn with the wrecks of lost manhood and womanhood, bordered with the graves of buried hopes, resounding ever with wailing and lamentation, leading onward and ever downward to endless night and bottomless despair. And Satan strews the first stages of this downward road with flowers, lays a thousand snares for your inexperienced feet, and reaches out his hundred hands to drag you to ruin.

In the name of the God of Shadrach, Meshach, and Abednego, in the name of your own eternal future, I urge you to choose the upward path. When tempted to commit an act unworthy of the sacred name you bear, to make cowardly concessions to popular clamor, to sacrifice the Right for the Advantageous; when Satan, raising any golden idol calls on you to bow down like the rest or pay the penalty: then, in that hour of trial, look back through the mist and shadow of twenty-three centuries and by the glowing light of that furnace seven times heated see those heroic faces, transfigured by the dauntless courage that shines from every feature, confronting the wrathful countenance of the monarch of Babylon; and sounding across the gulf of time that lies between, ringing clear above trumpet and harp and dulcimer, rising clear above the multitudinous noises of idol worship that roll across the crowded plain of Dura, listen to those words of triumphant faith, "Our God whom we serve is able to deliver us," and of triumphant courage born of that triumphant faith, "But if not, be it known unto thee, O king, that we will not serve thy gods nor worship the golden image thou hast set up"!

Luther before the Diet of Worms

No HISTORY, whether it be of an individual, a nation, or the world at large, runs from age to age with steady flow. Often the whole current of human thought and action, bursting the dykes of long-established usage, seeks a new and broader channel. At such critical moments the destinies of nations hang trembling in the balance. As a myriad rays of light gather from the sunglass into one dazzling focus, so towards one of these momentous periods a thousand streaming lines of history converge, and issuing thence, carry through distant centuries the light and heat of that fiery center.

It is one of these brilliant focal points, shining like a star on the far-off horizon of the Middle Ages, that I have chosen as my theme. Not, with elaborate argument, to discuss and compare its complex relations of cause and effect; that is the lofty labor of the profound essayist, of the philosophic historian.

Mine is a simpler yet more congenial task: to rescue from the mist and shadow of a half-forgotten century one of the most thrilling pictures in the Book of Time; to paint on the glowing canvas of the present a historic scene, now fading from our sight, at which all Europe once gazed with bated breath; and to trace the converging currents of history which invested that scene with such profound significance.

And truly, in all the varied panorama of the past, what picture, save one, is worthier of Titian's glowing colors or the majestic genius of Michelangelo? In the city of Worms, on that memorable April day four hundred years ago, a new world, standing face to face with the Old World's pomp and power, flung down the gage of irreconcilable battle. In the earthquake throes of the revolution there inaugurated, the foundations of the ancient social and religious order were upheaved, and the mightiest despotism that ever swayed the destinies of Europe tottered towards its fall.

To understand the true significance of this meeting and the vast issues at stake, let us look back a moment over the more remote past and watch the tide of European history, now ebbing, now flowing, but ever rolling onward toward that momentous conflict.

Almost the same period in the history of our globe witnessed the rising of the two mightiest powers that have ever yet borne sway over its inhabitants. The first of these was Imperial Rome. Like the rising waters of a flood the resistless ever-encroaching tide of Roman conquest swallowed up, one by one, the nations of the ancient world. The walls of her giant rival, Carthage, fell crashing to the ground. The Greek valor, which had immortalized the names of Marathon and Plataea, availed nothing against this new antagonist. Persia and Asia Minor, Syria and Palestine, Gaul and Spain, even far-off Albion, fell before the might of Roman arms, till war ceased for lack of further foes. Bound hand and foot, the captive nations lay helpless at the feet of the conqueror, and Augustus Caesar, seated on the throne of the world, received the homage due to God alone.

During this lull in the tempest of war, this calm of utter despair that followed utter defeat, the star of the second and more wondrous empire rose in beauty over the sleeping plains of Bethlehem.

And Heaven drew nearer Earth that night,
  Flung wide her pearly portals;
Sent forth, from all her realms of light,
  Her radiant immortals.

They hovered in the golden air,
  Their golden censors swinging,
And woke the drowsy shepherds there
  With their seraphic singing.

Age after age shall roll away,
  But on Time's rapid river
That shining star's celestial ray
  Shall never cease to quiver.

It was but a little child, born in a stable, cradled in a manger, in the smallest hamlet of a despised and enslaved nation; yet around that birthday revolve the ponderous wheels of human history. It was but a homely and obscure event, unnoticed amid the turmoil of those troubled times; yet on that long-sought fulcrum rests the Archimedean lever that moves the planet today. Towards it, through countless ages, set the currents of the ancient world; from it rolls that ceaseless stream of influence which is the hope and glory of the new.

From the lips and life of that Gallilean carpenter a new and strange force went forth to conquer the world. "Truths that wake to perish never" began their onward march. A bloodless banner floated at last among the gory battle flags of ancient Rome and gathered a devoted army beneath its snowy folds.

Never had the warlike nations of antiquity prepared to resist so strange an invasion. No belted warrior led these marching columns to the attack; it was the Prince of Peace Himself. Without sword or shield or military discipline or earthly leader; unheralded by burst of martial music or stately tramp of armies; silent, swift, resistless as the oncoming of the morning light, that strange skirmish line moved upon Rome itself.

The Eternal City recognized its mortal foe. She summoned to her aid all the savage enginery of war, the weapons of hate and scorn, the wild beasts of Africa, the pomp of martial power, the tortures of the rack and stake. But what mortal weapons can defeat immortal Truth or resist immortal Love? The bodies of its votaries were torn limb from limb, their voices were drowned in smoke and flame, their ashes scattered to the winds of heaven.

But the sacred Truth for which they died issued from the flames, fresh in the vigor of eternal youth, radiant in the splendor of immortal beauty, without the smell of fire upon her shining raiment. Above the crackling of the martyr's pile, the howl of savage beasts, the roar of angry multitudes, the echoes of her compelling voice rang on from soul to soul, gathering ever fresh adherents from the ranks of her enemies, till pagan Rome, the mightiest structure of the ancient world, fell to rise no more, and the followers of the humble Nazarene mounted the throne of the Caesars.

Yet, alas! the hour of outward triumph marked the beginning of inward decadence. The splendor of the Roman name, the thousand memories of Roman conquest, the old Roman lust for world-wide dominion, proved a fatal inheritance to the followers of the Prince of Peace.

From the mailed hand of the falling giant, Christianity snatched the Roman sword that had so long held the world in awe. The genius of her successive leaders forged fresh fetters for the captive nations of Europe, and in after years reduced them to a servitude of which the Roman Caesars never dreamed. They had ruled only the body. Their direst vengeance had stopped its pursuit at the grave. This new Caesar claimed absolute dominion over body, mind, and immortal soul. His blessing opened the golden gates of an endless heaven; his awful anathema followed the despairing victim through all eternity, dragging him forever into still deeper abysses of anguish. Like some massive fortress, this sacerdotal empire lifted its ramparts to heaven itself and buried its foundations among the deepest hopes and fears of the human heart. When Martin Luther first saw the light on the plains of Eisleben, the tempests of a thousand stormy years had dashed in vain against its mighty buttresses.

Yet even then, in the very meridian of papal glory, the silent forces of decay were already undermining the colossal structure in which its haughty inmates deemed themselves secure. Once more a spirit of deep unrest among the nations threatened the imperial power of Rome. The sighs of millions held in spiritual bondage, like the moanings of the troubled sea that cannot rest, swept in saddening murmurs over Europe. Through wintry centuries this surging sea of miserable humanity had been fast bound by the fetters of a pitiless tyranny. Now, at last, a strange mysterious warmth, as of coming summer, was piercing those frost-locked depths, and ten thousand hearts were vibrating to the thrilling summons.

For three years this beacon light of resistance to spiritual oppression blazed on the plains of Saxony, till answering fires began to glow throughout Germany, to shed their light from the great University of Paris, to gleam from mountaintop to mountaintop in freedom-loving Switzerland. Ulrich von Hutton, the Demosthenes of Germany, hurled his fiery philippics against the oppressor; the poet-shoemaker of Nuremberg consecrated his lyre to the spreading of religious truth among the poor and ignorant. Reuchlin and Erasmus had given back the long-hidden Word of God to the scholars of Europe; while from his fortress of Wittenberg Luther thundered against the fundamental doctrines of the papacy.

But by this time awakened Rome, long disdaining to enter the lists against so humble an antagonist, recognized her danger. The storm which had been muttering over the Seven Hills burst in fury on the head of the bold reformer, and the thunderbolt of the Papal anathema was launched against him from the Vatican. For many centuries that awful curse had blasted all on whom it fell; yet to complete her triumph and his ruin Rome summoned to the great Diet of Worms the power and royalty of Europe and summoned her rebellious priest to appear before that magnificent tribunal, publicly retract his errors, and humbly bow once more beneath her sovereign sway.

So all the roads that led to Worms glittered with flashing armor and echoed to the tread of princely retinues; while to meet them and his fate, weak and sick in body but of heroic soul, came the lonely monk of Wittenberg. Thus the slow-moving currents of history whose course we have been tracing brought at last, face to face in the great Hall of Worms, the monk, with his pen and scholar's gown, and the Colossus of the medieval world.

And now look back, through the envious shadows gathering over that distant time, and tell me: what possible element of interest, attractiveness, or grandeur is wanting in that historic scene?

Does the eye delight to linger on scenes of earthly splendor, the gleam of gilded armor, the pomp and pageantry of regal power? Count the royal banners floating in that vast audience hall. Never before has so proud an array of kings and princes been gathered together on European soil. Probably never in human history has any orator addressed an audience more imposing in its magnificence and power than that which waits to hear the recantation of the recreant monk of Wittenberg.

Do you admire physical courage? Does your heart burn

and your pulse throb at sight of a hero boldly facing overwhelming odds? Then measure the strength of the giant that humble priest so dauntlessly defies.

The haughty Emperor of Germany once rebelled against the yoke of sacerdotal Rome. His cries and tears, as he stood three days and nights in the snow, barefooted and in beggar's rags, at the gates of the castle of Canossa humbly imploring pardon of the sovereign pontiff within, told all Europe of his utter defeat and bitter humiliation.

John Hus had raised aloft the banner of religious freedom and gathered thousands to his standard; yet the vengeance of Rome destroyed him and drenched the fair plains of Bohemia with the life-blood of his followers. Savonarola's trumpet tones rang through Italy itself like the clang of fire bells in the night; yet purity of purpose and lofty courage and prophetic eloquence and civil power and hosts of loyal friends availed not against the iron hand of the world's master. The lightning stroke of papal wrath laid in ruins the structure the patriot-priest had so painfully built, and in the flame and smoke of martyrdom his brave soul returned to the God who gave it.

These are the scenes of horror that rise from the tomb of the past, like visions of the sheeted dead, and crowd upon Martin Luther's memory, yet fail to shake his steadfast soul.

Do you seek a higher, nobler courage than mere contempt of personal danger? Then bow in reverent homage before the moral heroism that shaven monk displays. On one hand life lies fair and full of the richest promise before him. Rome holds out her glittering rewards. There is no pinnacle of ecclesiastical power he may not attain. No dream of human ambition is too fair for him to cherish.

Yet at the call of duty he has chosen another and a sterner path; has forfeited the sympathy of his own kindred; has made himself an outcast from the church in which he was born; has incurred the enmity of the powerful, the thunders of the Vatican, the bitter hate of his past associates; and now, alone among his enemies, he faces the ignominy of a traitor's death!

But does the philosophic mind demand a deeper cause of interest than the courage or character or destiny of any single hero? Then look beyond these combatants, and in awestruck silence recognize the mighty forces that have here met in deadly conflict. The most far-reaching revolution of modern times has begun its course. On that glittering arena the Old Order and the New stand face to face: the Old with its barbaric magnificence, its fixed social forms, its weapons of war and bloodshed; the New with its freedom and light, its spirit of investigation, its quenchless love of liberty.

The University is here arrayed against the Court, learning against despotic ignorance, reason and argument against the sword, the battle-axe, and the stake, the force of ideas against the force of arms.

His is the voice of religious liberty, protesting against ecclesiastical despotism, of independent thought against mental slavery, of heartfelt spiritual worship against soulless rites and outward forms.

Haughty Emperor of the West, Nuncio of the Roman Pontiff, electors, kings, and princes, born of an age of war and bloodshed, you cannot realize the power of these invisible forces that are swaying the world of humanity around you. Vain are your serried lines of battle and storms of shot and shell against the silent onset of new ideas, the resistless march of eternal Truth. Your petty courts and armies fill the air with noise and clatter. In the majesty of an awful silence moves the mighty enginery of Heaven, and the earth moves her darkened continents toward the sunlight of a new day.

It is no mere rebel priest that confronts the splendor of your power and dares the lightning of your wrath. Shake from your blinded eyes the scales of sense and outward things. Wake to a higher, a deeper, a spiritual vision, and see your vain pomp and glittering grandeur fade before the august assembly gathered around that apostate excommunicated monk of Wittenberg!

From countless graves of violence and blood the holy martyrs have risen to defend the cause for which they died. Not now in the agonies of torture, forsaken, betrayed; but radiant with the joy and peace of eternal triumph, the raging flames of martyrdom now weaving a fadeless aureole about their heads.

Luther alone? defenseless? among his enemies? Ten thousand loving hearts are bearing his name to heaven on the wings of prayer. Truth and Justice stand, like mighty viewless sentinels, at his side. Around him throngs this silent army of the sainted dead:

> And, beyond the dim unknown,
>   Standeth God within the shadow,
> Keeping watch about His own.

From those martyred dying hands he caught the banner which he holds aloft today. His own may be stricken from its staff; his voice, like theirs, stilled in death, yet what glorious visions come crowding on his prophet's soul!

Down the long vista of coming centuries he sees those sacred folds advancing, reeling in the shock of war, rent by storms of persecution, reddened, alas! in the life-blood of its brave defenders, darkened oft-times by shadows of spiritual declension, till at last, in the depths of that far-off future, they float in triumphant beauty over land and sea.

Now, the bitter chill, the twilight darkness of the dawning; then, the meridan warmth, the unclouded splendor of that new day for which

> Our blind world, staggering on its round of pain,
>   Has so long watched and waited.

With the brightness of that new day shining in his face, with the glory of that coming triumph thrilling in his soul, Martin Luther turns to the grand tribunal, which holds his life in its hands, and makes his calm, immortal answer:

"I can and will retract nothing; for it is not right for a man to speak against his conscience. Here I am: God help me: I cannot do otherwise!"

The sixteenth century has long since mingled with the irrevocable past. The thunder of its cannon, the groans of its oppressed, the cries of its victims, the fierce clamor of its battlefields, the Babel of its myriad voices, sank long ago into eternal silence. Kind nature, with the returning verdure of countless summers, has hidden from our sight the last traces of its million bloody graves. A thousand of its heroes, who thought their fame as lasting and secure as the solid earth on which they trod, have been swallowed up by pitiless oblivion.

Yet, through the battle-smoke and dust of conflict that roll their eddying folds across that troubled century, we still see one heroic face, alight with heaven-born courage; one lonely monkish figure towers aloft, erect and firm against its background of turbulence and war; and rising clear and strong above the din of battle and noise of falling empires, ringing across the seething gulf of time that lies between us and that historic day, we still can hear the music of that calm and fearless voice, and catch the ringing echoes of those heroic words.

The flag which Martin Luther held aloft floats today over whole continents the Roman eagles never knew; the cause for which Martin Luther labored still works its miracles among the hearts of men; and as the stately procession of the centuries passes in silent majesty by that hero's grave, each owns its deep indebtedness, and casts thereon its tribute laurel of gratitude and love.

A Twentieth Century Alliance—Business and Religion

PSALMS I AND XV

BEFORE THIS GATHERING of influential citizens I come as a practical citizen myself, the head of an educational organization employing millions of capital, whose operations extend over the whole United States.* I come also as an educator, whose sublime task and inspiring opportunity is the training, the molding, and the inspiration of those who are themselves to form and guide the civilization of tomorrow.

I come, in the third place, as a soldier of the common good, passionately devoted to our great Republic and its democratic ideals, keenly interested in current events and tendencies, and eager to fight the wrong and encourage the right as our groping, stumbling, bewildered civilization struggles upward toward the light.

And, most vital and important of all, I come to take and give counsel as a Christian, believing with all my heart in the fatherhood of God and the brotherhood of man, and in the redeeming grace of our Lord Jesus Christ as the one threefold remedy for our sin-sick, suffering, and bloodstained world.

Our human civilization, like some mighty ship, freighted low with her precious cargo, is today, alas! afloat on stormy seas, and everywhere men's hearts are failing them for fear of the total wreckage of our present and future. But we who

---

* Dr. Smith is speaking of Washington and Lee University.

trust in God can look out on our tempest-driven world with serene and steadfast hope, knowing that infinite Love is at the helm and the divine Purpose standeth sure.

With cool courage, therefore, and with unshaken confidence, let us make a study of the winds and currents that are sweeping us onward in this marvelous age of revolt, world-wide warfare, and universal reconstruction. Like some giant pendulum our civilization is today swinging from an age of authority, docility, and stabilized institutions into a new age of almost appalling democracy and fluidity, of revolt against law and tradition, of freedom from every external control.

Because it was so sorely needed and was so long and so cruelly suppressed, this revolt will undoubtedly swing too far in the direction of anarchy. Much that is valuable is already being undermined and destroyed, and for a time there will be great disorder, confusion, loss of property, and distress of mind.

But as sure as God reigns, the gains will in the end outweigh the losses, and the new Christian era, when it finally reaches its equilibrium, will be saner, wiser, and happier than the past has ever been. Instead, therefore, of joining the world-wide chorus of lamentation over the moral laxity and devilish cruelty of this transition period, let us study its more hopeful aspects.

In what direction are the great tidal currents of religious thought sweeping us? What are the dominant characteristics of this new religious era upon which we are evidently entering? By studying the "signs of the times" our judgments may be clarified, our needless fears lightened, our duties made clear, our efforts made more confident and effective.

I will briefly describe five of the outstanding characteristics of twentieth-century religion as distinguished from the religion of our fathers and grandfathers. These are:

First, A New Emphasis.

The church of the Middle Ages and of the Reformation emphasized truth rather than conduct. They seemed to fear and fight error rather than sin. They tried to exterminate heresy, as religion's chief enemy, with fire, and torch, and sword. It was an age of carefully-wrought-out creeds, of systematic theology, of endless warfare over questions of interpretation and belief rather than questions of life and conduct. Each different interpretation of any part of the Bible seemed of such importance as to make a new denomination necessary, and as no two students of the Bible can possibly agree on all Biblical teachings, this process of continual subdivision filled Protestant Christendom with warring sects, quarreling vehemently over the process of baptism, the divine decrees, the administration of the Lord's Supper, church music, ordination, the second coming, and all similar questions of Biblical interpretation.

During the past half-century a vast world-wide humanitarian movement has shifted the religious emphasis from theology to life, from creeds to conduct, from intellectual beliefs to daily behavior. You cannot interest the congregations of today in abstract theology nor divide them into warring camps over predestination and modes of baptism. Whether we rejoice in the change or deplore it, it is clearly evident that the church of today fears sin more than error, and considers wickedness a worse foe than heresy.

Of course right conduct should spring from right beliefs. Both are essential to perfect Christianity. But undoubtedly our fathers overemphasized theology and overvalued slight differences of belief. The first notable characteristic of today's religion is its emphasis on conduct rather than on creed.

Second, a New Method—that of co-operation rather than competition.

The chief obstacle to the spread of Christ's kingdom on earth has been the quarrels of its friends rather than the assaults of its foes. The various battalions of the Lord's army have not only never made a united effort against their common foe, but have filled the earth with blood and tears and hatred fighting one another. The very growth of Christian zeal, under these circumstances, must intensify such inter-Christian hatreds and split the church into ever-increasing and ever-warring fragments.

During the last two generations a marvelous and wonder-working change in Christian spirit and working methods is ushering in a new era of Christian co-operation, with the controlling emphasis on life and conduct, on which they all agree.

When a drunken, diseased, ragged, hungry outcast stumbles into a rescue home, if the all-important question in his case is what religious views he shall be taught, no two denominations can unite in his service. But all enthusiastically agree and can work together in healing his diseases, giving him food and clothing, finding him a good job, and teaching him to be sober, reliable, truthful, honest, and industrious.

The shifting of religious emphasis from creedal beliefs to Christian conduct has inaugurated a world-wide series of interdenominational enterprises, has retaught the Church its essential unity in Christ, and is everywhere bringing Christians of every name and kind more closely together in life and work and thought.

And since organization is the genius and miracle-worker of our amazing age, it is now for the first time becoming possible to organize the whole body of Christians into a world war against war, slavery, oppression, national cruelties, and heathenism, thus changing the whole attitude of the non-Christian world toward Christ and His religion.

Third, a New Recognition on the part of the non-Christian world of the worth and value of religion to the individual, to the community, and to the nation as a whole.

The nineteenth century was the age of scientific research, of marvelous inventions, of the intoxicating accumulation of new-found wealth. Its scholars turned with ardor from theology and metaphysics to the study of nature's laws. Its inventors harnessed nature's forces. Its manufacturers distributed even to the humblest undreamed-of material comforts. Its industrial leaders exploited the helpless. Its economists deified dividends. Its educators believed and taught that book-learning for everybody would solve both civic and moral problems.

The age became frankly and openly materialistic, looking with scorn on religion as a thing apart from life, an outgrown system of abstract beliefs. A thousand voices during my boyhood predicted its speedy decay and disappearance.

Through bitter experience civilization has learned since then that learning and wealth and material comforts, instead of making men good, merely increase their selfishness and power of evil unless sanctified by religion; that science and art and inventive genius may give to man the superhuman power of devils but cannot make him loving and unselfish.

Even the non-Christian world has been appalled during recent years at the murderous wickedness of mankind without the mollifying influence of Christianity, at the utter inability of mere culture to curb the lust and cruelty of unregenerate human nature.

Surely it was through the over-ruling of a divine Providence that at this critical period of doubt and despair the spiritual forces of Christianity, now at last becoming united and practical, concentrated their energy upon the very problem which science and invention had failed to solve, the superhuman task of making men's hearts and conduct what they ought to be.

No wonder, therefore, that today, all over the world, statesmen and legislators, economists and financiers and business leaders, great newspapers, luncheon clubs and chambers of commerce, are realizing for the first time the value and necessity of spiritual forces, are openly proclaiming that only a widespread practical revival of religion can save modern civilization from speedy ruin.

And so has come about what would have seemed to our grandfathers incredible, that is:

Fourth, a New Alliance, never dreamed of in any former age, between idealistic Religion on the one side and practical Business on the other.

The real World War, compared with which all other world wars are but skirmishes, is the never-ending and world-wide conflict between Good and Evil. The most difficult attack ever undertaken by human forces is the invasion and conquest of the heathen nations by the militant forces of Christianity. The biggest business enterprise on earth today, whose billions of capital and millions of workers and world-wide operations make the Steel Trust and Standard Oil look like corner groceries, is the conquest for Christ, body, mind, and spirit, of the whole human race.

The Christian business leaders of yesterday could never get enthusiastic about theological discussions or wearing white robes and playing harps forever on the other side. So they left religion mainly to women and children and to white-haired men too old to work, and plunged with redoubled ardor into money-making, never dreaming that the Lord's causes were even then in greater need of consecrated business leaders than of learned theologians.

Today the whole atmosphere has changed. Business reaching up towards God and religion affecting the daily life of men are meeting at last on common ground and are everywhere joining their forces to do God's work in the world. This should make an unconquerable alliance, the unselfish idealism of the prophet and interpreter yoked with and utilizing the trained brains, the limitless resources, and the all-conquering energy of twentieth-century business.

It is dedicating to the work of God not only money but all the wonder-working forces of steam and steel and electricity, the auto and the airplane, radium and the X-ray, the radio and the movie-film, sanitation and medicine, agriculture and engineering—all are being dedicated to God and utilized in the King's urgent business.

Surely it was by the divine ordering and not man's purpose or wisdom that, in this hour of the world's appalling need, religion and business should join hands to rebuild our war-shattered world, when even the existence of Christian civilization seems imperiled.

And surely I need not say that with religion made more businesslike and business made more Christlike I confidently predict:

Fifth, a New Christian Era, marred, I do not doubt, by many faults and inconsistencies, as in the past, but far outdoing the past in advancing the Kingdom of God on earth.

The new Christian era will be experimental, no doubt, often too engrossed in social service to lift its eyes and soul to heaven, yet on the whole a wonderful period of world-wide conflict with the works of the devil, of vast Christian unified organizations and enterprises, of the ever-increasing consecration of business men and business money to the service of God and man combined.

The very fluidity and confusion of this war-shaken age, while increasing religion's peril, has trebled her opportunity. Never in recent centuries has the church of God been so united, so zealous, so increasingly militant, as she is today and will be tomorrow.

Let us, as from some Mount of Vision, rededicate ourselves to the great task of making the Church militant the Church Triumphant.

"The Heavens Declare the Glory of God"

PSALM XIX:1

THE MOST SUBLIME and far-reaching word in all the vocabulary of earth and of heaven is the name of the creative Spirit which we call God. Tell me just what the word God means to any human being, and I can tell you at once his character here and his destiny hereafter. As a man's vision of God expands it lifts him above the pettiness and debasement of earth, fills his soul with unutterable sublimity, and brings him into close kinship with prophets, apostles, and martyrs who have trod those heights before him.

For the attainment of this understanding of God, the most sublime of all studies, there are only two textbooks, His Word and His works. His blessed Word tells us of His limitless love and His redeeming grace, through the sacrifice of His Son. The starry heavens declare His glory, and echo, through all their myriad worlds, to the thunder of His power.

Let us stand, then, for a while, with uncovered head and reverent heart, in the great temple of Nature, open the second volume of God's revelation, and read the inspiring testimony of the stars to the glory of their Creator.

The inconceivable Age of the stellar universe gives a new and deeper meaning to the eternity of God.

We say that God is a spirit, infinite, eternal, and unchangeable; but, measuring our human history by a few centuries, we catch not even a glimpse of the true meaning of this one of

God's attributes. The study of the history of even our tiny little world, which is still in the early morning of its life, brings us face to face with such millenniums of time that all human history seems but a fleeting moment.

Through countless ages we can trace His almighty hand forming our earth for the abode of men; back through long ages of plant and animal life; then through infinite aeons of time before life was created, ages of fire and flood, tidal wave and ice sheet, earthquake and volcanic outburst, still recorded in the earth's structure; then through the infinite ages when the earth was without form and void, till human thought staggers under the weight of the Infinite.

Then, from this vision of our little world, lift your eyes to our giant sun and his billions of companions sweeping in blazing glory along their celestial pathways, and remember that to their hoary antiquity our little world is but a newcomer among the hosts of heaven. Then tell me if the heavens have not told you something of the eternity of their Creator.

The Unchangeableness of the heavens reveals another of God's mighty attributes and thus declares His glory.

Everything on earth bears the stamp of constant change, speedy decay, inevitable death. The changing seasons, the waning moon, the setting sun, the falling leaf, the fading flower—these are but types of all things earthly. The smiles of today are tears tomorrow; the faces that brighten our life are hid in the dust of the grave; the scenes that charm our senses most prove to be dissolving views; brilliant promises end in nonperformance; disenchantment poisons every pleasure; a secret bitterness is mingled with every cup of joy;

> Stars that shine and fall,
> The flower that droops in springing,
> These, alas! are types of all
> To which our hearts are clinging.

Amid all these shifting scenes, these blighted hopes, these sad farewells of our transient life, the soul of man yearns with unutterable longing for something solid, permanent, and abiding. In such an earthly environment it is hard to realize that there is One above us who is the same yesterday, today, and forever. From the dizzy whirl of earth and its shifting panorama it rests and steadies the very soul to lift our thoughts to the steadfast glory of the starry heavens.

Those silent stars looked down on Abraham as he journeyed to the land of Canaan, on David as he tended his sheep in the wilderness, and on the sleeping plains of Bethlehem when their light paled before the radiance of a new star. They have seen the rise and fall of Babylon and Nineveh, of Egypt and Assyria, of Greece and Rome; the rushing tide of time has undermined the empires of earth, cast down its mightiest dynasties, swept away whole races of men, and swallowed up one by one the civilizations of the ancient world.

Yet the mighty enginery of the starry heavens rolls on unchanged; the shining Pleiades and belted Orion which stirred the soul of Job on the plains of Uz are looking down on the ceaseless bustle of New York and Chicago; and when our boasted civilization has gone the way of its predecessors and our modern republics and world-wide empires have become mere names in a half-forgotten past, these same constellations will be rolling in stately splendor across the midnight sky and telling to races now unborn the glory of their unchangeable Creator.

The sublime Magnitude of the universe bears striking testimony to the glory of its Creator and Ruler. Even our little family of worlds, with the sun as its blazing center, is itself of an awe-inspiring extent. Eight worlds besides our earth whirl incessantly around the mighty sun which holds them all in their fixed orbits by its resistless attraction, and each of these has from one to a dozen moons whirling around it as a center.

Our earth is one of the nearer worlds, yet it is ninety-three million miles away from the sun. This distance is almost unimaginable. A rifle ball would take nine years to bridge this gulf of space. Yet Pluto, the furthest member of the sun's family, is nearly forty times as far. Picture to yourself the stupendous size of this group of planets with their encircling moons all whirling round the sun. And then learn that the whole solar system is a mere point of space in the universe; that the nearest of all the billions of fixed stars twinkling over our heads is eight hundred thousand times as far as our sun.

The size and number of these whirling worlds is beyond the human imagination. Our tiny earth is eight thousand miles through and weighs six sextillions of tons. Yet it is flying around the sun at the rate of over a thousand miles a minute. Two of the other planets are a thousand times as large as the earth, and the giant sun is over a million times as large. Yet our sun is but one of over a hundred billion constituting our Milky Way Universe, and with our modern telescopes we can locate hundreds of other universes scattered at almost infinite distances through the depths of space.

These brief statements have but touched the circumference of our subject. None but a trained astronomer can even begin to comprehend the complexity and glory of the stellar systems or the size and number of their constituent parts.

Now go out under the gleaming heavens and remember that these gleaming stars are vast suns like ours, many of them thousands of times as large, with their cataracts of fire and whirlwinds of flame, sweeping in majestic silence along their appointed orbits, and you will begin to catch a faint echo of the thunder of His power, who created every one and hurled it forth on its awful journey.

The Machinery of the starry heavens reveals the infinite wisdom of its Creator. This universe is concrete Thought saturated with Mind. It is the very glory of our human intellects to catch glimpses of the eternal Mind and follow infinite Wisdom even a little way into the unknown.

Let me mention but five instances of such wisdom and foresight in preparing our little world, so that it alone, of all our family of planets, can sustain animal and vegetable life. And remember that the greatest invention is the one that accomplishes the most complex and astounding result by the simplest means.

Number One: The marvelous Succession of the Seasons, the varied phenomena of spring and summer, of fall and winter, giving endless variety to all climates, to all vegetation, and to all human experience, is produced by giving a slight tilt of twenty-three degrees to the axis of the earth, instead of having it move exactly at right angles to its plane of movement around the sun.

Number Two: The endless Succession of Day and Night, with their alternation of activity and rest, with the glories of morning and evening, which are essential to human growth, activity, and efficiency, is produced by the simple device of giving the earth a whirling motion on its own axis, as a top is spun by the fingers. Such whirling motion is not necessary to a planet.

Number Three: Giving Fresh Air to every breathing animal on the face of the globe.

Every living animal feeds every moment on the oxygen of the air, breathing in oxygen and exhaling carbonic acid gas which can no longer support life. The simple device of *making warm air expand,* not only carries the exhaled air away from the breather but also causes the circulation of air all over the globe, furnishing every animal, wherever it is located, an abundance of unused air at all times.

Number Four: Making every green leaf of all vegetation an ever-acting Air Purifier.

Every living animal breathes in oxygen and breathes out carbonic acid gas which can no longer sustain animal life. Every green leaf of every living plant, through the influence of daylight, takes in carbonic acid gas, absorbs the carbon to build its structure, and throws back the oxygen into the atmosphere to be breathed in again by animals. Thus all green vegetation is continually purifying the air for animals to breathe and every breathing animal is continually breathing out carbonic acid gas which is the necessary food of all vegetation.

Number Five: Perhaps an even more amazing result is produced in the health, sanitation, and maintenance of life all over our earth by giving to our oceans of surface water on the globe the property of evaporating and condensing at ordinary earth temperatures. This property causes the distribution of vapor and rains all over the globe. But for this simple and marvelous device there could be no rains, no rivers, no dew, no snow—no possibility of sanitation, no fresh water anywhere on the globe; for it is evaporation that changes salt water into fresh.

In all this we stand amazed at the might of God, His infinite power, His unimaginable skill; but in all of this complex nature around us there is no note of fatherhood, no voice of love. It is a spectacle of all-embracing, pitiless force, of inexorable law; myriads of vast suns rolling on their predetermined pathway toward annihilation and death.

It is when to this revelation of His work we add the blessed message of His Word that the reverent heart learns the true nature of Deity; that this irresistible Power is making all things work together for our good; that this infinite Wisdom is promised for our guidance, our protection, our limitless development; that this ineffable Love may be our daily companion, our support in trial, our comfort in sorrow, our glorious reward in the eternal life to come.

Thus does our vision of God become well-rounded and symmetrical, our awe and admiration balanced by love and gratitude. Then and then only does God himself become an inspiration, his companionship our chief earthly blessing, the knowledge of Him our happiness here below and our glory in the world to come.

V
America Today and Tomorrow

In March, 1904, the General Assembly of Virginia resolved to celebrate the hundredth anniversary of the Peace of 1812 by presenting to the Government and people of Great Britain a bronze replica of the Houdon statue of George Washington. The bronze replica was made, but the World War prevented its transmission.

In 1921 the Virginia Legislature took up the matter again, sent the bronze replica to London, and appointed a Committee of four, consisting of the Governor, the Lieutenant Governor, the Speaker of the House, and the Clerk of the Assembly, with such members of their families as they might select, to go to England and formally present and unveil the statue.

The English Government cabled that they had set up the statue in Trafalgar Square, that the unveiling would be on June 30th, that beginning on June 24th the whole party would be the official guests of Great Britain for eight days, and that the Governor or his representative would be officially rated as a Crown Prince during the period of entertainment.

As the Governor could not go, he appointed the President of Washington and Lee as his official representative. The whole party, with several wives and children, numbered nine. They were placed in most luxurious suites in the Carlton hotel, furnished with an official social guide to instruct them as to dress and behavior, with their own special table and waiters, and with four cars always at their disposal.

Every day of the eight was full of stately functions, a formal reception by the King and Queen, another by the Prince of Wales, banquets and luncheons by Lady Astor, Lady Markham, the City of London, the University of Oxford, and others.

After the address of presentation the Marquis of Curzon replied, accepting the statue, with twenty Confederate and Union veterans grouped directly in front of the speaker.

Virginia's Gift and Message to Great Britain

SEVEN LONG and eventful years ago, that she might fittingly celebrate the close of a century of unbroken peace and give expression to her equally unbroken friendship, the Commonwealth of Virginia, by the unanimous action of her legislature, resolved to present to the government and people of Great Britain this bronze statue of her most illustrious son.

Little did she realize, in those days of deceptive tranquillity, that the resistless forces of world development were even then preparing another and sublimer celebration—and culmination—of that century of peace.

Little did we dream that before our tribute of love could cross the seas our ancient friendship would be re-cemented and glorified by comradeship in suffering and partnership in noble deeds.

Those early days of 1914 seem already strange and mythical and far away. A world-wide and aggressive campaign of slander and detraction, re-enforced by the success of German competition and the results of the Boer War, had produced a world-wide feeling of uneasiness as to England's future. Even her friends had begun to wonder whether there might not be some truth in the confident German assertion that long years of ease and sloth and luxury had rotted out the old English heart of oak and disintegrated the bonds that held her vast and polyglot empire together.

Yet here, as often in similar times of crisis, the amazing and incredible happened, when the normal and expected would have bankrupted civilization.

The swift and marvelous awakening of the old English spirit at its best, eager for every imaginable sacrifice; the stubborn heroism and amazing unity of her whole population; the scientific skill and inconceivable speed with which all England was transformed into a vast military workshop; the revelation of inventive genius and scientific efficiency and resistless energy never dreamed of before; the splendid and passionate loyalty with which her far-flung colonies swarmed across the seas and threw themselves into the fires of hell to save their imperiled Motherland—this no human wisdom could have predicted, no mere logic can account for. It was a modern miracle wrought as of old by the will and purpose of almighty God, the affirmative answer of the human spirit to the call of the divine.

And as the true meaning and vast issues of the mighty conflict slowly revealed themselves to the American people a no less amazing drama was enacted on our side of the Atlantic.

A stubbornly isolated and peace-loving nation, her politics often dominated by English-hating hyphenates, her intellectuals kneeling with unanimous devotion at the shrine of German culture, her whole people fattening beyond imagination on the profits of other peoples' wars—this was the America transformed almost overnight into a nation of a hundred million war crusaders, her domestic quarrels forgotten, her hyphens obliterated, her war profits cast aside, her whole people from the lakes to the gulf on fire with a fury of battle-ardor and a unanimity of self-sacrifice never known before in American history—this was the long-delayed but glorious answer of America to the call of the world's need.

But of deeper significance to humanity than this spiritual

rebirth of England and America has been their celebration of a hundred years of peace by the heartfelt renewal of their ancient and unforgotten kinship.

When German militarism, nurtured to giant strength and satanic ferocity, was hacking its bloody way through France and Belgium, when the night of medieval tyranny seemed settling back upon the earth, when the hopes and institutions and blood-bought liberties of Anglo-Saxon civilization hung trembling in the balance, then these two great Anglo-Saxon empires, waked by the spirit of God as from an evil dream, realized their essential unity, the littleness of their past and present differences, the height and depth and strength of their old-time kinship. Fighting and dying side by side they learned, for all time, we trust, that blood—warm, living, sacrificial brothers' blood—is thicker far than water.

It was a kindly Providence, therefore, that by delaying Virginia's gift has so glorified and hallowed it. And surely no commission was ever entrusted with a more precious token, a more urgent plea, or a more congenial message.

Its chairman is a most unworthy spokesman, yet there is a certain fitness in his selection, for he represents an institution of learning whose history is interwoven from the beginning with that of Washington and of the old colonial days when England and America were one.

Founded in 1774 under the British crown, it was deliberately chosen by George Washington to bear his name and utilize his wealth that learning might temper and uplift his country's new-found liberty.

After the wreck and ruin of the Civil War it was refounded and rebuilt by Washington's great kinsman, the immortal leader of the Confederate armies, who, having no money, gave himself to the institution and endowed it forever with his matchless example, his sacred dust, and his incomparable name.

Across its velvet lawn the benignant figure of Washington looks down upon the chapel and tomb of Lee.

Within that sacred shrine, on the right of Virginia's holy of holies, is Peale's splendid portrait of George Washington in the scarlet uniform of a British officer as he fought with Braddock. On the left is the majestic figure of his fellow-rebel, Robert Edward Lee, in full Confederate gray. And over each regal head, their battlefields forgotten in a common homage to the mighty dead, droops a cluster of glorious flags, all dear to Virginia's heart: the stars and bars of the vanished Confederacy, that hallowed flag of memory and tears, the stars and stripes of the re-United States, with not a rent remaining, and the meteor flag of England, the world's chief symbol and promoter of law and ordered liberty. Outgrown antagonisms, forgotten enmities, temporary defeats, apparent disloyalties, transient and unimportant political alignments, all submerged in a higher allegiance, all bearing witness to the essential unity and magnanimity of the Anglo-Saxon race, its ability to forgive without forgetting, its innate reverence for the supremacy of the individual conscience over all lesser loyalties!

VIRGINIA'S GIFT

It is in the spirit of this hallowed shrine that Virginia has selected the gift that accompanies her message of love.

In this spirit as her messengers we hereby present to the Government and People of Great Britain this bronze likeness of one who forsook her flag, rejected her sovereignty, and fought against her king. And with splendid and characteristic magnanimity she answers the challenge by placing this one-time rebel on a pedestal amid the mighty monuments and memories of Trafalgar Square.

Glory of English art,* the gathered treasures of a thousand

---

*The site of the Washington statue is immediately in front of the National Gallery, near the monuments to Lord Nelson and Edith Cavell.

years of culture; glory of English manhood, with stirring memories of Copenhagen and Trafalgar and the Nile; greater glory of English womanhood, gladly dying in loneliness and obscurity, that her country's cause might live!

A tiny bit of bronze in this goodly company, yet it represents the best Virginia has to give, the flower and fruit of our Western civilization, the embodiment of our Anglo-Saxon ideals of manhood and character, that immortal product of English ancestry and American rearing, George Washington, Founder and Father of our American Republic!

In his matchless character were combined and concentrated the qualities and characteristics of both England and America at their best. In habitual reserve, assured authority, and quick resentment of personal indignities he was an English aristocrat of the highest type. Yet among naked savages and wilderness pioneers his ready fellowship and cordial American democracy made him a universal favorite. His English love of home was only equaled by his American devotion to little children.

A knightly cavalier and polished courtier in social circles, he was from his very boyhood a rigid Puritan in sobriety, chastity, and uncompromising fidelity to duty.

His Anglo-Virginian hospitality, free and openhanded to the verge of extravagance, was made possible by his energy in business affairs and his executive ability as a money-maker.

A soldier from his youth, lifted to the heights of military glory, he ever hated war and subordinated the military to the civil power.

To the dogged courage and grim determination of his fighting English forbears he added the impetuous daring and quick resourcefulness of the American pioneer.

The splendid leadership with which he won his country's independence was, if possible, surpassed by the patience and diplomatic skill and farseeing statesmanship with which, through toilsome and trying years, he solved the problems and laid the foundations of the new republic.

And when to these is added his purity of motive, his entire freedom from selfishness and personal ambition, his lofty serenity in times of defeat and disaster, and his sublime and unwavering trust in a higher power, no wonder that he seems set apart as a superior being, hardly formed of human clay.

As such a character enriches and ennobles the whole world, so does such a memorial add luster and distinction even to Trafalgar Square. And as these restless tides of cosmopolitan humanity ebb and flow through this throbbing heart of England's empire, may these Anglo-Saxon monuments, now and forever, teach to a groping and bewildered world this uplifting Anglo-Saxon lesson:

That all true greatness, whether of an individual or of a nation, is always and forever *moral,* never merely material; that the ultimate test and unerring measure of human civilization is not its wealth or commerce, but the characters it produces; that the most momentous question confronting Britain and America today is not what we have or what we will get, but what we are and what our children will become.

VIRGINIA'S MESSAGE

This is Virginia's glorius gift to Great Britain, and with Virginia's gift goes her whole heart. Her messengers are but a tiny group, lost amid the swarming thousands hurrying across the Atlantic, and she speaks through a single insignificant human voice, scarce heard among the devilish cries of hate that fill the world today, but they are the messengers and messages of love, the only rebuilder of our wrecked and prostrate world.

And love, in spite of its temporary eclipse, is still omnipotent and eternal, the sweetest thing in the world, the most contagious thing in the world, the mightiest thing in the world; and as earth's restless oceans swing to and fro to the changing moon, so shall earth's restless millions yet ebb and flow responsive to her divine control.

It is in fulfilment of this high mission that we bring to the government and people of Great Britain assurance of the undivided fellowship and ever-increasing friendship, not only of our beloved Virginia, mother of states and statesmen, but of the equally undivided South, and of the great body of our American citizens from the Atlantic to the Pacific. We confidently assure you that the shrill cries of hate you sometimes hear are but the clamor of a narrow and turbulent shore-line, not the voice of the great deep that lies beyond.

We rejoice that a thousand ties are every day binding more closely together our gigantic and peace-loving democracies.

With our unmatched English tongue, now clearly destined to become the chief treasury and vehicle of the world's civilization; with our wealth of English literature, centering in and radiating from our blessed English Bible; with our common reverance for the purity of womanhood, the sanctity of the home, and the rights of the weak; with our common admiration for unselfishness and the spirit of service, our universal Anglo-Saxon instinct for justice and passion for liberty, our common recognition of the imperative of conscience, the rights of the individual, the fatherhood of God, and the essential brotherhood of man—with these multiplied and mighty bonds, so recently softened in the furnace of a common suffering and welded anew on the hard anvil of war, this is a world friendship that has come to stay, and may the God of England and America doom to speedy destruction every effort and agency that attempts to weaken or undermine it.

To this assurance of abiding friendship, in which all America joins, Virginia would add, to her sorrowing and heavy-laden motherland, a message of sympathy and hope peculiarly her own. She too has known the hellish aftermath of war, its shattered industries, its new-made graves, its appalling problems of social and economic reconstruction.

Her present happiness and prosperity confirm these inspiring truths, which she learned amid the chaos and sorrows of 1865 and would share with the sorely stricken England of 1921: that the money and ships and machinery destroyed by war are not the essentials or permanent treasures of human civilization but only its tools and trappings, already on their way to the scrap heap; that a nation's richest assets are the faith and courage and constancy of its citizens; that while vegetables grow best in sunshine and balmy air, these finer growths of manhood and womanhood are blighted by too much sun and multiply without limit in times of storm and darkness.

In these invisible but priceless assets, piled high in the bank of heaven, England is today immeasurably rich, in spite of her huge debts and tragic losses; and they will yet, as in Virginia's case, bear ample dividends of future peace and wealth and happiness to heal the wounds of war.

VIRGINIA'S PLEA

But friendly messages, however sincere, cannot salvage the wreckage of world-wide war, nor can memorials to the dead, however imposing, heal the wounds and solve the problems of the living. For love is barren and friendship but an empty word if they are not translated into practical helpfulness.

Let me, therefore, representing not only my own beloved State and the thinking millions of America, but the heart and hope of a troubled world, add to our words of love this urgent plea—*That the English-speaking nations of the world, so recently united in war, unite again for the more complex tasks of peace, and in closest and most unselfish co-operation, enter at once upon a joint program of world leadership and reconstruction.*

As an active participant in the great movement, I positively affirm that it was neither hate nor fear that swept our peace-loving nation into war, but a tidal wave of moral indignation that would not allow us to stand idly by and see civilization murdered before our eyes. Our millions crossed the ocean with the consecrated zeal of crusaders going to the rescue of the holy sepulchre. Those were days when selfishness and greed dissappeared in the pure white flame of an altar fire. Would God that the English-speaking nations might rise again and forever to those lofty heights of international co-operation for the common good!

Long since has mankind learned the value of the Golden Rule in the crowded life of a community; that selfish individualism defeats its own ends; that sacrifice for others enriches both giver and receiver. We are now learning in a thousand forms of co-operative industry that the Golden Rule is also good business, that selfish and self-seeking individualism is the road to failure, that friendly co-operation increases the productivity and happiness of all.

Why should these priceless lessons, learned at the cost of long years of individual and business warfare, be thrown aside in the fields of international politics? Why should the English-speaking nations, with a wrecked world to be rebuilt, stand idly and selfishly and ineffectively apart till the fires of anarchy make their task impossible? Surely never in human history has an imperial race been confronted with such a combination of manifest fitness and sublime opportunity.

Even amid the devastation of the world war, not a single English-speaking nation has seen its government overthrown, its territory ravaged, or its economic machinery wrecked by revolution. As a group they are industrially more able to rebuild the world than ever in their history.

They are today incomparably the wealthiest group of nations in the history of the world. In spite of their individual debts and losses they probably hold more wealth at their disposal today than before the war—wealth which, if wisely invested, could both lift a bankrupt world into profitable production and at the same time still further enrich its owners.

Their power today in world politics is as conspicuous as their wealth. If united in a common purpose no power on earth could seriously hinder, far less successfully oppose, their joint program. And they are not only at peace with each other, but are warm friends and recent allies, with a common language for immediate and universal intercommunication.

They are also, as a group, the most enlightened, scientific, and progressive of all the nations of the earth, owning and controlling the great inventions which have given to mere man almost supernatural powers.

With a common racial kinship, a common religion, and similar ideals of character and conduct, obeying the same general code of laws, accustomed to the same modes of self-government, and utilizing the same methods of business organization, they constitute today the most homogeneous group of nations ever known on earth.

Their instinct for justice and fair play, their universal capacity for sympathy and pity, their habitual generosity and regard for the weak, their religion of brotherhood and unselfish service, and their long and successful experience in guiding and developing backward races—all these, as if by the planning of divine wisdom, have especially fitted the Anglo-Saxon nations for rehabilitating a wrecked and bewildered world.

For over four hundred years, gathering irresistible momentum, modern civilization has been swinging from the intolerable despotism of the Middle Ages toward universal democracy. Amid world-wide tumult and incessant revolt, the power hitherto wielded by the few has been steadily tranferred to the many in ever-widening circles. As long as the diffusion of intelligence and morality kept pace with this rapid diffusion of power, the sum total of human welfare and happiness steadily increased with the progress of democracy till the very name became a religion.

But the furious actions and reactions of the World War checked all the processes of education and religion, unchained everywhere the devils of hate and greed and cruelty, and hurled the millions back toward savagery, while at the same time, by shattering all forms and institutions of human authority, it transferred to these unprepared millions the fatal gifts of power without knowledge and liberty without self-control.

In this imminent crisis the Anglo-Saxon nations, and these alone, are able to teach these groping and experimenting masses the true meaning of democracy.

Their specialty is combining liberty with law, diffusing intelligence among all classes, subordinating military to civil authority, and training all to attain their ends by argument rather than by force, while they alone, of all earth's races, have the present power to arrest the processes of destruction and hold these restless millions in check till they and their nascent governments have gained experience and stability.

We boast of our Anglo-Saxon capacity for organization. Why not use it for this most stupendous of all tasks?

We are proud of our economic wisdom and scientific efficiency. Why shall we go on talking war and building battleships for a world that is homeless and naked and famine-stricken? Why not prove our claims and fill our coffers by manufacturing and distributing what earth's millions want?

We claim to lead the world in the difficult art of ordered and law-abiding self-government. Why can we not teach and guide these bewildered millions and save them from impending self-destruction?

Amid these stately memorials of our heroic dead who gave their lives for others, let Christian England and Christian America, with unshaken confidence in the ultimate triumph of righteousness, rededicate themselves to the advancement of human welfare.

That increasing intercommunication should increase international hatred; that the gains of research and the wonders of invention should be forever prostituted to the arts of murder; that we should bankrupt ourselves paying war's dread tuition fees of blood and tears and taxes, yet with childish obstinacy refuse to learn her lesson; that we should with endless and futile toil save and build that war may waste and destroy, and stagger to our daily tasks under its hellish and unnecessary burdens; that we should forever rear our homes and cities for the torch and our precious children for the slaughter-pen—this is the sum of all human folly and wickedness. It is unreasonable, unthinkable, intolerable; and with the help of our newly enfranchised womanhood shall yet be made impossible.

The art of co-operative self-government in and among our huge and crowded populations shall yet emerge from its crude and experimental infancy. Our giant newborn democracies shall yet outgrow this child-era of unreasoning fickleness and credulous ignorance and infantile hysteria, and become mature and sane and wise and self-controlled.

The present clouds and darkness are the morning not the evening twilight of our human civilization. In spite of morning clouds and morning storms and the crude incompleteness of morning work, the spirit of national friendship and co-operation is working its daily miracles among the hearts of men, and this old earth of ours, battle-scarred, crime-stained, tear-drenched, tempest-tossed, and never more tempest-tossed and tear-drenched than now, is yet rolling her darkened continents out of our present hatreds and horrors toward that blessed though far-off noonday, when love and brotherhood shall be the law of human life, and sacrifice and service the test and measure of human greatness.

What Is the Matter with Christendom?

To EVEN the most casual observer our modern Christian civilization is just now seriously threatened with disintegration. During its two thousand years of steady evolution certain Christian nations such as those in northern Europe, the British Isles, and North America, have surpassed all others in inventive genius, in organizing ability, in constant efforts toward human betterment, in widely-diffused education, and in moral culture.

But today the majority of these advanced nations have been wrecked by constant and murderous warfare, their young men slain on countless battlefields, their homeless millions starving and in blind revolts, and their statesmen and rulers at their wit's end.

Industrially these hitherto prosperous nations have seen their busy cities laid waste, their factories and railways and power plants destroyed, and their governments overwhelmed by colossal debts. The war between capital and labor seems growing ever fiercer, while the primitive savagery of the underworld is everywhere rising in rebellion against the control of the intelligent few.

We have thus seen our whole world drenched in blood, rent by racial hatreds, and vainly striving to unite in friendship and brotherhood.

Surely it is time for every intelligent American of every race and party to attempt a diagnosis of our ailing world that we may apply some remedy before it is everlastingly too late. What, then, *is* the matter with Christendom? What has caused this appalling backset in human civilization, which a half-century ago seemed to be progressing so favorably?

In endeavoring to answer this vital question I will first mention minor contributing causes. Then I will describe three great revolutionary movements, which, working in parallel, have brought our modern world into such a crisis of world-wide warfare and bankruptcy.

Of the three minor causes the first is the biological regression of our most favored families. As the superior individuals of our competitive world climb the ladder of fame and success, they cease rearing children, and thus slowly extinguish our leading families, while the scrub families continue rearing abundant progeny of this lower grade. It was mainly by this process of gradual deterioration that the great civilizations of antiquity slowly disintegrated and were overthrown.

The second of these minor causes is the weakening of the old religious restraints on our animal natures and appetites. Today to increasing millions the horrors of hell fire and the glories of heaven are subjects of jest rather than spiritual realities with a powerful influence on conduct.

The third and the last of these minor causes of unrest and revolt is the swift increase of wealth, of leisure, and of recreation among all classes. A toiling world, intent on getting the next day's food, is too constantly busy to be dangerous. It is the widespread leisure and spare cash, aided by religious retrogression, that are undermining those moral restraints which constitute the very core of Christian living.

These three, however important, are but minor causes of civilization's breakdown, local whirlpools in the three greater tidal currents which must be stemmed to save the ship of modern civilization from future shipwreck.

The three greater causes are essentially psychologic, having to do with man's moral and intellectual nature. His body has long ago become standardized. Its powers and faculties are incapable of any revolutionary improvements. The field of human progress, now and in the far future, lies in man's moral and emotional nature.

Of the three great problems which we must solve to avoid human bankruptcy the first and most important may be worded as follows: *man's mastery and control of his environment has far outrun his mastery of himself.*

The past century has witnessed an almost explosive development of man's knowledge of natural laws and hence of man's power, but with no such corresponding development of his moral and social nature.

The life of an unclothed tropical savage, living in his hut and hunting his food from day to day, makes almost no demands on his moral or social nature nor on his capacity for organized co-operation.

So a serf or slave, working under hourly restraint and compulsion, with neither liberty nor leisure, can live his life and perform his tasks with very little development of his moral or social nature.

The most elementary steps in modern civilization, however, such as permanent mating, town-building, grain-planting, the raising of domestic animals, the care of dependent children, the hiring and management of subordinates—all these originate and develop moral and social powers and faculties far in advance of those of the solitary savage or the owned slave.

Every added increment, however, of liberty, privilege, wealth, or power demands for its right use and control a corresponding advance in morality, wisdom, and self-control, or man cannot control wisely these added powers.

During the last hundred years the social and moral agencies of Christendom have spent their energies in national hatreds and bloody warfare, while the forces of advancing knowledge and applied science and inventive genius have given to earth's millions an increase of wealth, leisure, and power never even imagined by their forefathers.

If man's moral and social nature had but kept pace with this knowledge and power, utilizing the forces of nature for the good of all; if the colossal expenditures of hate had been invested in the service of love, the civilized nations of Christendom would by now have lifted their people to such heights of culture, comfort, health, and widely-diffused happiness as were never approached or even imagined in all the ages of the past.

Instead of this we are today immersed in an earth-wide flood of hatred, murder, and human misery never known before in human history.

The second of the three main causes of human misery is the retention, as the basic working principle of human evolution, of the ancient *Law of the Jungle,* called in modern scientific phrase, *the Survival of the Fittest.*

This principle holds that constant warfare, the crushing of the weaker by the stronger, is the natural and therefore the universal law of human progress.

This doctrine that Might makes Right gained wide scientific acceptance just as the might of the strong and their engines of wholesale destruction were increasing beyond the imagination of all former tyrants and robbers. Universal warfare, under the politer title of competition, thus legalized and enthroned, became the accepted law of human relationship.

Competitive religion, concentrating its emphasis on interpretation and theology, rather than conduct and brotherhood, divided all Christendom into warring sects and drenched the earth with tears and blood.

Competitive business split every industry into warring

enterprises, organized labor and capital into hostile armies, and led every nation to fly the pirate's flag with endless tariffs and subsidies and international trade-wars.

Competitive racialism has been even more destructive of human love and human brotherhood. Lynchings and Ku-Klux clans at home, pogroms and massacres abroad, have bred hatreds and jealousies and social ostracism between white and black, Protestant and Catholic, Jew and Gentile, native and foreigner, all over Christendom. And competitive nationalism, elevated into a religious creed by Germany and Japan, has so filled the world with fears and hatreds that at last jungle law and jungle theory culminated in the carnivals of jungle practice known as the First and Second World Wars.

A Christian civilization can no more be based on universal legalized warfare than world-wide commerce on legalized piracy, domestic business on legalized robbery, or home government on legalized rebellion.

Christ abrogated the law of the jungle and substituted the law of human brotherhood, and if his Christian civilization is to escape the fate of its pagan predecessors, it must abandon its pagan practices and substitute in home and world industry and commerce the principle of friendly co-operation for that of competitive warfare.

The third cause of civilization's present plight is undoubtedly *the premature triumph of democracy.*

The distinguishing feature of modern history is the vast all-embracing democratic movement which originated as a reaction from the intolerable tyranny of the Middle Ages and has for four centuries been steadily transforming human civilization.

This movement has been essentially successive diffusion among the Many of the powers and privileges hitherto monopolized by the Few: first, the diffusion of religious liberty and privilege; second, of political liberty and governmental power; third, of knowledge and educational training; fourth, of wealth and leisure and industrial power.

As no human hands surrender wealth or privilege or authority without a struggle, the spread of democracy has been a long succession of revolutions, a spreading revolt of the masses, their claims increasing with every victory, their struggle renewed after every defeat, till all must now agree that among the nations of Christendom the day of autocracy is over, the ultimate triumph of democracy near at hand. Whether for weal or woe the Christian civilization of the next era is to be overwhelmingly democratic.

Let it be noted, however, that this process of diffusion, to be safe and successful, must be two-fold: not only a diffusion of power and liberty of action among the many, but also of moral culture that will enable the many to use their power wisely and unselfishly.

Until recently the advance of democracy throughout Christendom was accompanied by a parallel increase of education and enlightenment and human welfare, so that belief in democracy became almost a religion, and it was generally anticipated that its world-wide triumph would usher in not only a new era of prosperity but with it a new era of universal brotherhood.

The rebellion, however, of two powerful nations with their tributaries against democracy and Christianity broke up this beneficent equilibrium between diffusing power and diffusing enlightenment and plunged humanity into two disastrous world wars.

The furious actions and reactions of these wars have reversed the normal growth of education and religion, have taught hatred and cruelty as a holy duty, and have desolated our world from one end to the other.

The overwhelming triumph, however, of the United Nations over the forces of tyranny, the inherent ability of Right to triumph over Wrong, the amazing resilience and resourcefulness of the human species, and the moral government of a God of Providence—these all justify us in anticipating with confidence an approaching era of human civilization which shall abandon warfare as a legitimate means of settling international controversies, and shall be juster, wiser, and more prosperous than any preceding era in human history.

Let all the lovers of humanity, therefore, unite in the rapid spread of the ideals of Christianity at home and abroad all round our troubled world. Let our newly-formed world organization receive the hearty support of every lover of human brotherhood.

Let the messengers of the Prince of Peace carry the Gospel to every heathen land. And let Christian America dedicate its vast wealth and industrial power and world-wide influence to the rebuilding and betterment of our war-torn world.

Some Things to Be Thankful for in the America of Today

WITH HIGH TAXES and with certain war deprivations some natural-born American grumblers are loudly longing for what they call "the good old times." Our purpose today is to describe the "good new times," to tell how doubly fortunate our land, America, is in this tumultuous period of human civilization.

In the near future our whole world, we trust, will be organized to abolish armed conflict among the nations, to compel every nation, large or small, to settle international quarrels before courts of justice and never again on fields of battle.

Our nation was dedicated at its birth to human freedom, justice, equality, and brotherhood. Even during our world wars it has been more free of wrecked cities, homeless wanderers, and starving citizens than almost any country on our war-torn globe.

American civilization is still far from perfect. It has grievous faults and many wide-spread injustices. But when I remember the America of my childhood and count over the vast improvements that have since then transformed our civilization, it so fills my heart with wonder and gratitude that I must share my feelings with my auditors.

Let us then very briefly recount some of the advances America has made and is now making during the past two generations of her history.

The first is our position as a world-power and the safety and security it gives us. In national unity and loyalty, in national wealth and prosperity, in international finance as the world's financial center, in international security from attack, and in international influence among all nations, our American Republic today leads the whole world, with no rival anywhere in sight. In such a period of world-wide disorganization following world-wide warfare, such national concord and international security should bring every Christian American to his knees in grateful thanksgiving.

Our second asset is our long-continued and unbroken industrial prosperity. Our land is strewn with busy factories, vast power plants, crowded highways and railroads, and millions of acres of growing crops. In accumulated wealth, bank deposits, and great industrial organizations all past records have been broken in the busy and prosperous America of today. And the rebuilding and refurnishing of a war-wrecked world will, I trust, keep our industries busy at full speed for many years to come.

A third asset is our present distribution of wealth among the lower classes. For the first time in our industrial history the wage-earning classes have been lifted to a new level of happiness and comfort by our industrial prosperity. To see millions of American factory hands driving every day to their work in their own autos, furnishing their homes with comforts and recreations never imagined before, investing their savings in stocks and bonds, and sending their children to first-class colleges and universities—surely this unprecedented distribution of our unprecedented income is a modern triumph of applied Christianity for which we should thank its divine Author.

The fourth of our national blessings is our increasing health and longer average life in America. During the past half-century the increasing skill and inventive genius of American physicians and surgeons have practically abolished three or four of our most prevalent epidemic diseases, have learned to cure others hitherto regarded as nearly always fatal, have distributed well-kept hospitals all over the United States, and are now concentrating their research on cancer, heart failure, the venereal diseases, and some other ills still unconquered. The advance in surgical skill has been equally marvelous.

These successive triumphs in the field of health and hygiene have so increased the average length of American life that instead of the forty years of the past century the average age of death in America is today from sixty-two to sixty-three years.

A fifth national blessing is the betterment and enrichment of country home life in every part of our vast Republic. Our American Christian civilization centers upon and radiates from the Home, and reaches its culmination in the ideal home circle.

During former generations our millions of country homes were left to loneliness and ignorance and isolation in the onward rush of our busy cities. Today the long-distance telephone and radio, the daily mail and rural free delivery, and above all the auto and truck and paved highway have opened to those isolated homes every city privilege, have carried into the country millions of city dwellers, and have sweetened and enriched country life beyond the imagination of the old-time country dwellers of former centuries.

A sixth blessing, never dreamed of by former generations, is the increasing freedom, social influence, and political power of American womanhood. It is hard for an American of today to realize the former legal helplessness of American womanhood and the many injustices the wives of that day suffered. The women of America today move on a different plane, and are honored, privileged, and protected as never before in human history.

At the same time the many labor-saving inventions and machines of today have so lightened the time-consuming functions of housekeeping and child-tending as to give the women of today far more time for recreation and various organized outside activities.

A seventh blessing is the increasing protection and care of helpless citizens, of the incurably ill, the blind and deaf and dumb, the insane or feeble-minded, orphan children, and the inmates of our jails and penitentiaries. We are steadily lessening the ills, improving the care, and lengthening the lives of these unfortunates of every grade and kind. It now makes us shudder to learn of their neglect, their utter helplessness, and their harsh treatment of only one or two generations ago. There is still much to be done, but at least we are steadily improving their lot.

The eighth asset has tranformed our social and industrial life in every state. It is the triumph of modern science in harnessing nature's forces to lift the burden of grinding labor from human shoulders. In all the past history of our human race all the so-called "lower classes" spent all their lives in grinding day labor. In very recent years science has harnessed the mighty forces of nature to do such work, leaving to man only the guiding of these wonderful machines. Steam power, water power, electric power, the power of burning coal or gasoline or fuel oil, all these together have given the working power of twenty-five horses, working day and night, for every single one of our one hundred and thirty-five million citizens. No words can describe what this is adding to the leisure, the happiness, and the general welfare of our citizens.

A ninth blessing, especially needed in this age of universal tension, is the swift increase of leisure and recreation among all classes. This is an era of numerous vacations and pleasure tours, of free reading-rooms and libraries, of camps and sea-beaches and crowded swimming pools, of great public parks and pleasure resorts, of innumerable movie theaters, of "teams" of every kind and contests without number. Never has "a good time" been in such easy reach of so many Americans of every age and kind. That the relentless grind of a mechanical and industrial age should be so sweetened and socialized and enriched is a combination of divine and human wisdom for which we can all give thanks.

A tenth blessing for which we should render heartfelt thanks is the recent marvelous development of transportation and intercommunication. The telephone and radio now scattered everywhere, the paved highways now reaching nearly every home, the auto flying below and the airplane above, the millions of printed messages carried every morning to every home and hamlet—this mighty enginery of intercommunication, knitting together all local clubs and local loyalties, seems specially designed by a kindly Providence to accomplish the impossible and weld even our multiform America into one Christian brotherhood from the Atlantic to the Pacific.

The next notable blessing to be mentioned is the nation-wide epidemic of educational zeal and liberality. America can rightfully boast of her gigantic industries and her rapid transportation. Never have American citizens enjoyed such wealth and leisure and daily privilege as they do today. But the most nation-wide and gigantic business in America is American Education, the right training of all her future citizens. It utilizes the most varied and stupendous plant, the largest income, and the largest army of employees of all American industries. With its numerous co-operating agencies it reaches more American homes and home circles than any other business.

During the past generation our educational agencies have been so broadened and enlarged as to reach all Americans of every age all the year round. Our former summer vacations are today given over to crowded summer schools. The American stay-at-homes are enrolled in vast Correspondence Schools, while free public libraries in every town and traveling libraries through the country are opening the gates of wisdom to every American citizen.

Another notable blessing, closely allied to education, is the recent nation-wide fraternal movement, a contagious epidemic of social and business brotherhood, a movement embracing both sexes and all ages, dissolving ancient social barriers, undermining ancient class enmities and religious prejudices, and knitting all Americans into one vast brotherhood.

The various religious and interdenominational clubs, the fraternal organizations in every college and university, the luncheon clubs like Rotary, Kiwanis, and the rest, the chambers of commerce and all similar business clubs, the social organizations of lawyers, preachers, and merchants, every kind and rank of women's clubs—these nation-wide social movements, affecting the whole nation, are steadily welding the whole American people into one vast brotherhood.

I will mention but one more of these transforming movements that are remolding our whole civilization. This is the rapidly developing Christian Unity movement. All over the United States the various denominations are drawing closer together. Many separate denominations have legally united into one body. Many others are debating such union, while interdenominational agencies and organizations are taking over many forms of Christian work all round the world. There is no question that the former separatism of Christ's followers is beginning to yield to the realization of the Saviour's longing that all his followers might be one.

Every one of these thirteen nation-wide movements is towards the betterment of our American civilization, the abolition of international hatreds and warfare, and the ultimate Christianization of our whole world. Let every true-hearted American, therefore, dedicate his heart, his mind, and his working-power to the attainment of these great ends.

The America of Today, Its Movements and Possibilities

OUR PLANET is still in its early formative period, not yet having reached its full maturity of either growth or function.

The human race on this maturing planet is still more recent, having been created long after the forming earth had been peopled with countless forms of plant and animal life.

Organized human civilization, following long ages of savage and tribal life, is at present in its earliest, chaotic, experimental infancy, swinging back and forth from one extreme to another in a rapid succession of temporary forms of civilization, such as the Greek, Persian, Roman, Hindoo, and Peruvian.

Our present tumultuous era marks the culmination of the contest between the despotism of the Middle Ages and the advancing democracy of the western world, leading, we trust in the near future, to a democratic government of the whole world and the abolition of war as a means of settling international disputes.

The five successive revolutions, now involving all the great divisions of former human privilege and activity and remaking modern civilization, constitute the subject of this discussion. The America of Today is in the grasp of these five interrelated and apparently irresistible movements. The America of Tomorrow will be the resultant, the complex product, of their complex warfare.

All five of them constitute distinct and successive elements in the vast epoch-making swing of the human pendulum from the prevalent medieval despotism of the One or the Few toward universal democracy, the ultimate enthronement of the Many. The world-wrecking tempests of two world wars constitute the final combat between ancient despotism and modern democracy, ending in the triumph of these five departments of progressive democracy, which are now, for weal or woe, reforming our modern civilization.

We are today in the perilous Age of Transition, swinging toward World Unity. That all of my readers, young and old, may gain at least a moving-picture knowledge of the seething currents of our American sea of life, let me give a momentary survey of each of these five sweeping movements toward a World Democracy of which our grandfathers never dreamed.

Let it be distinctly understood that in this verbal picture of the whirlwind conflicts and currents of the America of Today I am in no sense whatever presenting personal opinions or personal preferences, still less personal arguments or propaganda.

The vast sweep and complexity of the field covered, the personal and partisan hostilities involved, the lack of time for the discussion of a single problem mentioned, compel me in such flashlight picturemaking to be neither a Democrat nor a Republican, neither a Protestant nor a Catholic, neither a fundamentalist nor a modernist, neither an old-fogy nor a progressive—only a flashlight projector, revealing facts and situations but not personal opinions or even preferences.

And let us all remember that a whirlwind rush of today or an epidemic reaction of tomorrow may change American conditions and prospects at a moment's notice.

THE DEMOCRATIZATION OF RELIGION

The first of these great movements in time and probably in human importance is the democratization of religion, the steady diffusion among the many of the religious privileges and powers held and exercised by the medieval few.

This rebellion against religious autocracy burst into its modern effervescence about five hundred years ago. Its battle cry was religious liberty, the right of the minority and of the individual to worship his God in his own way. Its typical hero was the protesting martyr dying at the stake or in the torture-chamber of religious autocracy. Under the leadership of Martin Luther, John Calvin, John Knox, and their associates and successors this contest for democracy in religion has filled the earth with blood and tears and incessant conflict and is today severely lessening the unity and harmony of America.

The world-wide Roman Catholic autocracy, aided by its Knights of Columbus and other organizations and utilizing long experience and unbroken unity, is making a determined effort to attain the moral and political leadership of America, and hence of future Christian civilization.

This crystallized movement of a strong and united religious minority is much aided by the division of the Protestant majority into numbers of competing and sometimes warring sects. Under our American two-party method of settling all governmental problems, a thoroughly organized minority can frequently win important victories over a disorganized majority and thus seize governmental authority at Washington.

Working against this result, however, is the very recent movement among all the Protestant denominations toward confederated unity in all sorts of interdenominational enterprises, even to the uniting of two or more separate denominations into a single one. The world-wide swing away from traditionalism is also weakening the American loyalty to party names and partisan enmities and friendships.

Surely all thoughtful Americans will agree that to maintain unselfish, appreciative, constructive civic brotherhood among the warring castes and classes and races of the composite America of Today and the World Civilization of Tomorrow is a most vital and urgent American problem of today and tomorrow.

THE DEMOCRATIZATION OF HUMAN GOVERNMENT

The second revolution, following hard on the first, is the democratization of human government, the transfer of legislative and governmental power from the hands of the One or of the Few to the hands of the steadily-increasing Many.

Its battle cry is liberty. Its typical hero is the patriot, the rebel, the revolutionist. As no human hands surrender power or authority except to superior force, its resistless progress has been marked by successive whirlwinds of revolution involving the downfall of thrones, dynasties, and orders of nobility among the crystallized autocracies of Europe.

Under flexible forms of authority like ours in the United States it has been marked by the steady extension and diffusion of the ruling ballot to all adult citizens regardless of race, social standing, property holding, sex, or civic preparation.

During the past generation of war-torn years we have seen in America a nation-wide epidemic of revolt of all classes, especially of the immature and the criminal, against every form of restraint and law-restriction. It seems to be dissolving the old-time authority of parents, teachers, and policemen, of church and state and family. What the outcome will be, whether the triumph of a genuine self-government among the many or a period of lawless anarchy and crime, is not within the province of a flashlight picture.

THE DEMOCRATIZATION OF WEALTH

The third phase of the onward sweep of triumphant democracy has been the democratization of wealth, the long-threatened industrial revolution. This movement, rising into special organized power with the advent of the steam engine and the modern factory, is apparently reaching its culmination in this age of rapid communication and world warfare. It is again the triumph of the Many over the Few.

Through a thousand militant organizations these hitherto exploited millions are endeavoring to wrest from the capitalists and employers their disproportionate share of the accumulated wealth and present income of the world of business and divide it more equally among the poverty-stricken masses. This tumultuous uprising of the Many Who Lack against the Few Who Have is in many parts of the world overturning governments and spreading to all lands.

THE DEMOCRATIZATION OF KNOWLEDGE

The fourth stage in the progress of universal democracy is the vast educational movement which, in more recent years, is transforming modern civilization. It is the democratization of knowledge, the diffusion among the many of the accumulated knowledge of the race, hitherto the distinctive possession of the learned and ruling classes.

This educational revolution is probably the most distinctive, and certainly may be made the most beneficent, of all the phases of advancing democracy. In the United States it is becoming a universal passion. Our vast and overcrowded universities, our hundreds of colleges and technical schools, our thousands of high schools and of graded, farm-life, and business schools, our crowded summer schools and lecture programs, our traveling libraries and nation-wide correspondence schools, the stream of government publications giving information on almost every subject, the clubs and reading circles in every community, the millions invested in new educational enterprises, and the endless flood of newspapers and magazines—all are but different phases of the one great educational movement which, beginning only a few generations ago, promises to become, next to providing food and shelter, the chief occupation of modern civilization.

THE DEMOCRATIZATION OF HAPPINESS

The fifth and latest-born of these great movements is the

social revolution, the democratization of happiness, the diffusion among the many of the comfort, leisure, health, and recreation hitherto never dreamed of as a possible possession of the toiling millions which our fathers called the laboring classes.

This movement is barely in its infancy, born with the advent of the twentieth century, but it is already giving a humanitarian bias to all our laws and customs. The protection of women and of children, the dispensaries and free hospitals and visiting nurses, the municipal camps and wading pools and playgrounds, the rapidly-increasing legislation for the protection of the weak, the helpless, and the unfortunate against those who would oppress or plunder them, the countless homes for the aged, the orphaned, and the incurably diseased in body or mind—all these are outgrowths of the new and revolutionary theory that every human being born into the world has a right to his full share of human happiness as well as to his share of religious privilege, political power, worldly wealth, and the accumulated knowledge of the race.

In a final survey of this composite whirlwind we can easily identify certain outstanding American movements:

In religion, an increasing emphasis on practical Christianity, social brotherhood, individual freedom, and interdenominational activities; a diminishing emphasis on creedalism, abstract theology, verbal inspiration, ecclesiastical authority, and all church government of opinion or conduct.

In politics, a diminishing loyalty to the two old parties, the steady rising of numerous lesser loyalties, the growing servility of legislators to home dictation, and the threatened breakdown of our ancient two-party system.

In commerce an increasing honesty, truthfulness, square-dealing, and regard for the "other fellow" in every transaction.

In social sex relationships, an effervescence of freedom,

sex knowledge, and companionship, an epidemic of rebellion against any sort of restraint, especially the permanence of the marriage-bond.

In industrial enterprises, a rising emphasis on human welfare and human happiness, with a steady betterment of the condition of all laborers and employees.

In social and community life, an increase of leisure, of spending-money, of leisure-time recreations and new modes of travel, of healthful outdoor games and restful outdoor life, thus creating an era of recreation never hitherto possible in human civilization.

In educating our future citizens, an outburst of zeal, liberality, and practical interest and an era of wide opportunity for all ambitious Americans have created an educational opportunity for everybody never dreamed of before in human history.

That such novel liberties and intoxicating pleasures have led to a corresponding outburst of crime and lawlessness among the immature and the criminal during this perilous era is a solemn fact which should awaken every true American to wise and patriotic activity in order that American character may remain sublimely equal to American liberty and American opportunity.

The United States of Tomorrow

BEGINNING WITH the Reformation, a tidal wave of advancing democracy began to weaken the religious and civic autocracies of the Middle Ages. One after another they were displaced or altered as the contagious passion for liberty and human rights stirred into action the awakened millions of Europe and America.

By the opening of the twentieth century the triumphant progress of democracy seemed destined for an international triumph, and many optimists predicted a new day of worldwide freedom and self-government.

The First World War, 1914-1918, involving twenty-nine nations, not only opposed this trend but for several years threatened to substitute despotism for democracy over the whole of Europe. By 1918, however, the invading German armies were driven back into Germany, their supplies of food severely diminished, and their morale undermined by skillful propaganda. This led to a general rebellion of soldiers and people, the flight of the Kaiser, the collapse of the war machine, and a short-lived republican form of German government.

The Second World War, originated by Germany and Japan, was a still more savage attempt to extinguish democracy in both Europe and Asia. With the help of the vast empire of Communist Russia, the united democratic nations of the world, headed by the United States and the British Empire, finally conquered and disarmed both these nations and their allies, and are now striving to form a world alliance to prevent future international wars.

It is now clearly evident that our world is passing through a revolutionary transition period in its history. All round the world conquered nations now liberated and the heathen nations hitherto under the protective guidance of some European power are clamoring for complete independence, and many of them preparing to fight for it.

There is no question that human civilization during the second half of the twentieth century will differ fundamentally from that of all past eras.

Let it be our task to take our bearings, to measure if we can the force and direction of these world currents, and especially their effect on our American civilization of tomorrow.

Two important facts constitute the background of our study and the basis of our predictions.

The first is that *all true human progress in self-government and human welfare must be made against the natural savagery and selfishness of human nature.*

It is like the movement of a hard-beset sailing vessel against an adverse wind, yet compelled to utilize the very wind whose constant pressure it must overcome and reverse. In this case direct progress in a straight line against the wind is impossible.

The skilled pilot swings the ship like some vast pendulum back and forth obliquely across the line toward his goal. With each swing he crosses the line a little further toward the goal. Every long time-wasting tack is therefore a distinct gain, and at last he reaches his haven even against an adverse wind.

So is it with the precious bark of Christian Civilization, working as it ever must against the winds and tides of fallen human nature. We may always expect it to follow the law of the pendulum, always forsaking the golden mean, never following the straight path, yet always, on every long and weary swing, finding itself a little nearer the shining harbor of its hopes.

The second preliminary fact is this: All mass-movements of human nature are such a complex of good and evil that any partisan observer, selecting facts as he desires, can find ample justification for either pessimism or optimism. Each of us, therefore, can at any time "view with alarm" or "point with pride" according to his ruling motive or perhaps his party affiliations.

In this discussion, therefore, I will endeavor to award neither praise nor blame, to express neither personal hopes nor fears, but to give, as far as I am able, a clear and uncolored picture of the great social movements which are now transforming in one or two generations the civilization of our fathers.

In this hurried survey I will omit the unbroken advance of scientific knowledge, however important, and will examine the rapid changes taking place in our civic and social life in the five great departments of human activity. In the hurried survey of such an immense field I will of course merely indicate the direction of these great movements, although each one temptingly invites enlargement.

IN POLITICS AND GOVERNMENT

In the complex department of government three epoch-making movements are now clearly evident.

The first is the steady sweep of human government from autocracy toward democracy during the last two hundred years, the transfer of governing power from a single despot or a chosen few to the great masses of the people. We might call the process the democratization of human government. The almost comical fate of the dignified presidential electors so carefully planned for when our government was first organized is threatening all leaders who are not elected by popular vote. Even after the people have elected their representatives to state or federal offices they are now continually telling them what side to take in every important issue. The government of tomorrow will be not by the legislators but through them by the people. The very recent extension of the voting privilege to all the women of the land, and the present plea to let boys of eighteen vote, are but two examples of the modern diffusion of political power.

The second is a revolutionary change in political methods. Our two-party system of government has many advantages which I will not stop to describe. It is slowly being altered by the political action of vast class organizations of labor unions, of capitalists, of farmers, of teachers, of ex-soldiers. These are every day becoming more class-conscious and more articulate, are abolishing state and sectional and party lines, and vastly complicating future elections.

The third is the rapid socializing of all democratic governments. This means giving all governments more and more power over the daily lives of the citizens. Local governments are now controlling the business, recreation, health, and daily life of every citizen in a way never dreamed of by our fathers, while the Federal government is doing the same thing in all sorts of interstate matters. At first glance this seems the exact reversal of the vast democratic movement. The United States of Tomorrow will see the liberties of the individual and of his family surrendered more and more to the municipal government, the local self-government of cities and counties surrendered to the State in matters of state-wide importance, and state's rights and state boundaries fading out more and more as the national government extends its control over nation-wide problems and enterprises.

IN EDUCATION

In education several dominant tendencies are shattering old ideals and curricula and are slowly shaping the far broader and more complex training of tomorrow.

The first change is a growing belief that the right training of its future citizens is the *supreme business* of a modern democracy, the only solution of its internal problems, and the best investment of its time and money. The schools, colleges, universities, and research centers in the America of Today will all be doubled in the America of Tomorrow.

The second revolutionary change will be the increasing practicality of the whole school system. The old idea of taking severe mental exercises merely for their own sake is rapidly giving place to actual training for successful American citizenship, plus some specialized skill either to earn a living or to broaden the outside interests and activities of the future citizen.

The third vital change will be the broadening and enrichment of the curriculum of our high schools and colleges. That a thorough knowledge of Greek, Latin, higher mathematics, and philosophy, the ideal of the A.B. of my boyhood, is a first-class college education is no longer believed by anybody. The high school and college students of tomorrow will all have courses in physiology and hygiene, and will have their bodily health, eating habits, and teeth cared for by regular experts, the present long summer vacations will be largely filled by all sorts of out-door and shop activities, and the lower schools will add all varieties of moral, manual, recreational, and industrial to the strictly mental training of yesterday.

IN RELIGION

In the realm of religion the socializing tendency of the age manifests itself in three principal directions.

The first is the shifting of religious emphasis from abstract theology to concrete life, from written creeds to human conduct.

The church of the Middle Ages was mainly concerned with keeping its doctrines pure. Its battleground was interpretation, its deadliest foe the heretic, its hero the defender of the faith. The Christians of today are hardly interested in the doctrinal differences for which the medieval church shed the blood of its opponents.

The Christian leaders of today are far more concerned with motives and deeds and modes of living than with theological differences; their chief aim is to transform human life; their weapons are not arguments but love and sympathy and service; their hero is not the highly-trained theologian but the inspirational reformer, who wakens multitudes to a life of consecrated service.

The second characteristic is another revulsion from the Christianity of the Middle Ages. It is an increasing emphasis on the social ideal in religion, the rapid decline of the monastic ideal.

The typical Christian of the Middle Ages withdrew himself from all intercourse with the world that he might keep himself pure, free from contamination, and in close fellowship with God.

Today organized religion is devoting itself to the service of others. Today personal holiness and communion with God are considered as means to an end, not the consummation of religious life. That end is the salvation and betterment of others. Every working church is today divided into dozens of close-knit "circles" each working for the good of others. Every church today has its busy dining halls, its children's clubrooms, sometimes its gymnasium or swimming pool or camp ground. The keynote of the religion of yesterday was personal holiness; the keynote of the religion of tomorrow will be social service.

These two religious movements are rightly called changes in religious emphasis. The third is the vast transformation in the organization and work of the Christian Church as a whole.

Theology is divisive. No two students can ever agree on

all the details of biblical interpretation. The former age of creeds was therefore an age of constant cleavage, of multiplying denominations, of endless antagonisms and religious warfare.

As the emphasis shifts from creeds to conduct we find ourselves entering upon a new era.

We can thank God that the era of religious competition is all round the world giving way to an era of religious cooperation and union. When the Christian emphasis shifts to conduct and service to others, the various branches of Christians find themselves very close together. All over the world we today see Christians of various names coming together in all sorts of interdenominational enterprises, in community churches, in the union of two or more denominations into one. The movement is too vast and varied to be more than mentioned, but it is already giving allied Christians greater power in almost every country on the globe.

IN BUSINESS

As in the case of politics and religion, the business of tomorrow will be far more socialized than in former eras of human history. Since these problems are too numerous for full description, I will merely mention six tendencies. First, the business of tomorrow will be far more under governmental control and regulation than in former times. Second, the vast organizations of laborers will in the future share officially in adjusting such problems as hours, wages, and vacations. Third, the great organizations of employers will work jointly with those of employees in settling matters affecting both. Fourth, the old age of employees, and probably also their medical and dental care, will be arranged for as part of their remuneration. Fifth, with the world nations linked together as never before, vast intercontinental business organizations will soon be formed under the regulation of the World Council. Sixth, the present protective tariff walls barring international trade will steadily decrease or be abolished.

IN SOCIAL AND DOMESTIC AFFAIRS

The marvelous changes in ease of transportation, prevalence of wealth, freer social intercourse, and the epidemic of organizing that has swept the country, added to the entrance of wives and mothers into political and industrial life, are rapidly altering the social and domestic customs and ideals of the past. A few of these will be mentioned to exhibit the general trend of the more important movements.

The first is the added importance, influence, and independence of the country's women in home, church, state, and business.

The American woman, already more than an inch taller than her nineteenth century predecessors, is rapidly developing what were once called the masculine qualities of will power, self-reliance, initiative, and civic leadership, and is losing her ancient characteristics of emotionalism, trustfulness, and pliability.

The second social characteristic of the present age is a growing recognition of the value, the rights, and the privileges of every child, regardless of the social, financial, or racial standing of its parents.

This discovery of the value of childhood and the emancipation of womanhood rank as the two leading contributions of the last half-century to the civilization of tomorrow.

A third social movement is the growing humanitarianism of our American civilization, unwillingness to inflict pain or endure the sight of human suffering. This is manifested by our growing impatience with our cruel jails and chain gangs and penitentiaries, our growing abandonment of the death penalty, and our growing care of the aged, the orphaned, the deaf, blind, or insane. This humanitarian movement is hastened by the rising influence of womanhood.

A fourth very important movement all over the United States is the rapid loosening of the marriage bonds.

In many localities the present-day divorces almost equal in number the marriages. The marriage bond in America is no longer regarded as a lifetime obligation. It is rather a matter of temporary enjoyment, much clouded and hampered by the possible birth of children.

The multiform divisions of the Protestant part of our population, the independence of each state in managing marriage and divorce, and the absorption of the whole population in two world wars have probably contributed to the general indifference of the American public to the many evils of divorce. No general movement to restore the sanctity of the marriage bond seems to have made any headway.

CONCLUSION

We have now glanced at some of the important movements giving birth to the American Civilization of Tomorrow.

The one-man tyranny of the Middle Ages has given way to the triumphant democracy of today. But this vast tidal current toward individual liberty has reached its limit and is becoming more and more co-operative in everything except government. Getting their start in the necessary despotism in everything military, the governments of tomorrow will rapidly increase their power over the individual in all matters of everyday life.

Whether this ultra-modern increase of governmental control will make the human swarm evolve like the government of a hive of bees, with all individualism willingly sacrificed for the common good, or whether the movement will be checked before it becomes harmful, no one can yet foretell.

In such complex human progress the optimist can "point with pride," the pessimist "view with alarm," the demagogue climb on the band wagon, the conservative put on the brakes, each according to his motives and temperament, as the sublime procession sweeps us onward into the unknown future.

As for me, let me record my conviction that as I have seen with my own eyes the sum-total of human happiness and human welfare steadily increasing since my childhood, and as I know from the records of history that the era of our fathers was happier and freer than those which preceded it, I now believe that our human civilization is in the morning, not the evening, of its earthly day; that in spite of morning clouds and morning storms and the crudeness of morning work, we are steadily advancing, however slowly, toward a warmer and happier and more fruitful noonday than our half-open morning eyes can now foresee.

Our Social Progress in the Next Generation

Our human civilization is today passing through an era of world-wide warfare, revolt, and reconstruction. Old opinions, creeds, standards, modes of government, social divisions, are everywhere breaking up, or rather are being thrown into a common melting pot, to recrystallize in the civilization of tomorrow.

In my thought these multiplied revolutionary movements are but parts of a single vast coherent movement, sweeping steadily in one direction, although creating countless eddies which travel temporarily from the main current.

In the constant strife in all legislative halls, in the widespread war of capital and labor, in growing trusts and great monopolies, in the revolt of the young against all restraint, in the world-wide wars of the past generation, in strife of tongues, strife of parties, strife of classes, strife of embattled armies—in all this complex movement we can discern the slow transformation of our former western civilization into the next era of co-operative democracy.

As the progress of the next generation is to be but the unfolding of this mighty drama, let us try to trace the nature, the motive-power, and the direction of the current and thence try to predict its future progress.

ITS ETHICAL FOUNDATION

This modern impulse toward democracy is not primarily either political or economic, but essentially ethical and moral.

Its ideals and principles were entirely unknown to the civilizations of antiquity. They were first promulgated on the plains of Galilee two thousand years ago by the Founder of Christianity and spread with amazing rapidity over Europe. Though warped by a large section of His followers into a despotism, many other divisions kept alive the true spirit of democracy through the night of the Middle Ages.

Rediscovered and reinterpreted by the leaders of the Reformation, they have for three hundred years constituted the chart and the motive power of the social-democratic movement which is now transforming our ideas of the scope and functions of "government" and reconstructing our human civilization on a new basis.

The doctrine of the worth, the immortality, and the dignity of every human soul, of its privilege of personal access to God and sonship with Him, of the inherent equality of all human beings before the divine Judge, of the possibility of eternal life and glory to the humblest without the intervention of king or priest—these revolutionary doctrines lift serf or peasant up to and beyond the level of the king. They originated modern democracy and sounded the knell of all hereditary despots and oligarchies and privileged classes.

Ever since the Reformation the vast unprivileged classes have been rising into fuller and more equal participation in human affairs. They claimed equal legal rights, and human slavery was doomed. Before their claim to equal political rights the thrones of the ancient world are falling, their long-established dynasties are crumbling, and despots and tyrants of every kind and grade are steadily losing power. They are claiming an equal share of wealth and leisure, and countless labor unions are struggling with their employers.

They are demanding the blessings of culture and knowledge, and in response a thousand temples of learning have been constructed and crowded with eager students. Countless millions have been poured into our great educational systems, free to all the people; and everywhere lecture bureaus, correspondence schools, public libraries, demonstration farms, radio courses, and every conceivable agency for diffusing information are busily at work, placing at the disposal of the Many the blessings of knowledge hitherto the priceless possession of the Few.

They are claiming immunity from disease, and everywhere free medical care, sanitary homes, non-malarial regions, and free hospital beds have been placed at their disposal; everywhere great health movements and campaigns are sweeping the country, with costly homes erected at public expense for the blind, the deaf, the aged, the feeble-minded, and the insane.

And now the lower classes and helpless minorities are claiming social justice. Our outgrown, crime-breeding, medieval system of treating crime and criminals, our crime-training jails and chain gangs and penitentiaries are all under fire and probably tottering to an early fall. The colored millions of our population, with the other ill-treated minorities, are all rising to claim their constitutional rights and to participate more actively in the activities and the rewards of modern civilization.

The first stage of this great movement from the fifteenth to the nineteenth century might be called the era of civil and religious liberty. Its hero was the patriot; its motto, "Sic semper tyrannis."

The second era grew naturally from the first. The human freedom of the eighteenth century begot human power and efficiency in the nineteenth. During this efficiency era man harnessed the forces of nature, evolved the factory and the corporation, and learned to utilize forces and accomplish tasks hitherto undreamed of.

The active principle of this era was unlimited competition,

the survival of the most fit; its hero was the inventor and the organizer; its result, the creation of vast wealth, many millionaires, and many creature comforts, the release from bodily labor.

In spite of its world-wide conflicts we have now in the twentieth century entered upon an entirely new era. Its dominant note will be, not human liberty nor human efficiency, but human fraternity. The new age will value people above things. Its hero will be the philanthropist, the altruist who sacrifices himself for others. Its motto will be the golden rule, enunciated so long ago by the Founder of our religion, and so long reverenced in theory while disregarded in practice.

Perhaps I may be too sanguine. Yet, watching the marvelous progress of the moral and spiritual forces at work all round the world in modern civilization, I cannot but believe that, as the nineteenth century was the Age of Applied Science, the twentieth will in future ages be known as the Age of Applied Christianity.

In spite, therefore, of world-wide wars and world-wide tumult and the confusion of modern civilization, I find myself an unquenchable optimist, believing with all my heart that in this blessed land of ours the Golden Age lies before us, not behind us.

But this Golden Age is not coming of its own accord. There are many dark spots to be cleansed, many rank injustices to be remedied, much ignorance to be enlightened, much poverty and suffering to be abolished.

EDUCATION IN THE NEXT GENERATION

The educational development of the past generation will achieve greater triumphs in the next, but the line of progress will be in a new direction. The past era of standardization, fixed curricula, and attempted uniformity will give place to an era of differentiation. The schools and school systems of the next generation will be marked by variety, elasticity, and adaptability. High school boards will revolt against the selfish and paralyzing tyranny of the college and university; practical educators will revolt against the present theory of our educational system that the chief end of study is to prepare for further study; school principals will revolt against a cast-iron curriculum dictated from above without reference to local needs; and long-suffering parents will revolt against the Sing-Sing lock step of an educational machine by which the exceptional minds are led into mischief through enforced idleness and the sub-normal minds to even more harmful idleness through inability and despair.

The new generation will think less of the school and more of the child, and will make its educational machinery fit its raw material rather than the reverse. The school of tomorrow will be adapted to the needs of its own community. The college and university of tomorow will exist for the training of the individual student, not the student body for the glory of Alma Mater.

When our high schools train for life and not for college entrance, when our colleges train for rich and fruitful citizenship and not for a graduate department, then the moral side of education will come into its own; our complex educational machinery will train children, not to know textbooks, but to be wise, good, happy, and efficient; and our schools fitted to our varied American life will be elastic, adaptable, resourceful, and free.

OUR RACIAL PROBLEM

The next generation should cultivate and diffuse a fairer, kinder, and more democratic attitude toward the Negro. We should habitually differentiate them from one another, should recognize and applaud genuine Negro leadership and be willing to entrust responsibility and yield self-government to Negro communities. We must cultivate among them social differentiation and recognize their "upper classes," thus encouraging right ambition and uplifting racial pride and personal self-respect rather than an acute and paralyzing sense of inferiority and injustice.

Our boasted Southern "chivalry," "honor," and "courtesy" toward the womanhood and childhood of our own race and station in life must grow ashamed of its callous indifference and frequent heartless cruelty toward the equally helpless womanhood and childhood of another race and station, and gain a new and broader view of human brotherhood and human duty. A quick sympathy for the weak and a passionate love of justice must see to it that before our magistrates, mayors, and police courts the friendless Negro shall stand on an equal footing with criminals of our own color.

Our children, we hope, will have the wisdom and the courage to recognize the inconsistency and hypocrisy of most of our professed passionate zeal for the purity of the white race in the South; a one-sided zeal that grows wild with hysteric indignation at the attack on our racial purity involved in the assault of a Negro on a white woman, yet views without protest a thousand degraded white men living in concubinage with Negro women and filling the land with half-breeds.

Let the clearer vision of the next generation recognize the fact that there can be no defense against racial amalgamation till our double standard of racial morals is done away with; till our racial enthusiasts realize that the child of a Negro mother and a white father is as much a hybrid as the child of a white mother and a Negro father, and our Southern chivalry believes in, encourages, and protects the virtue of Negro womanhood.

I find myself leaning more and more to the separation of Negro communities from white ones, not primarily for the comfort or protection of the white families, but as the only means of developing self-government and community self-respect, with the growth of a "leading citizen" class, among the Negroes themselves.

THE ORGANIZATION OF RURAL LIFE

The next generation will undoubtedly concentrate its attention upon the better organization of rural life. The difficulties in the way of the betterment of rural life are many and formidable: monotony, isolation, bad roads, lack of capital, of leisure, of social life, of educational advantages.

And all these difficulties are doubled by the fact that our bi-racial rural sections must develop and sustain two complete systems of religious, social, and educational institutions to serve the population of the same territory.

The keynote of the new rural life will be organization, its method will be co-operation, its spirit the Golden Rule, its agents the church, the school, and the social center.

OUR TREATMENT OF THE ANTISOCIAL

Our age has not yet applied its new scientific knowledge to the treatment of crime and criminals. Our system of fines, of the virtual imprisonment of the poor for debt and of the accused for safekeeping, our methods of breeding and multiplying the number and the venom of the criminal class, our prisons and chain gangs and penitentiaries, all these methods are already a century behind our pedagogy, psychology, and hygiene.

Our own generation has already reached the stage of widespread and thorough dissatisfaction with the whole system. A new spirit of sympathy and fellow feeling for the antisocial is pervading all classes, and long before this new century has run its course our present repressive and punitive methods of dealing with crime will be outgrown and abandoned. The triumphs of research, expert diagnosis, and preventive medicine in the realm of public health will be repeated in the domain of public morals. Our children will learn that in crime as in other things an ounce of prevention is worth a ton of vengeance.

A NEW SOCIAL EMPHASIS

The former generations in the United States, especially, I think, in the South and West, have overvalued or at least overemphasized, individual rights, local self-government, and personal liberty. This was a natural inheritance from the old days of tyranny. Now it is everywhere retarding the spread of the co-operative democracy of tomorrow. Defiant individualism must give way to social harmony and co-operation. We must think more of the rights of others and less of our own.

In former ages we became saturated with the doctrine that to give everyone full personal freedom will make all free, that unrestricted competition leads to prosperity for all, that he is governed best who is governed least.

All these are false in the new era of co-operative citizenship, of the voluntary surrender of individual rights and liberties for the sake of still greater social liberty, social justice, social efficiency, and social happiness. The miracles of the twentieth century will be in the training of the young, the care of the unfit and the antisocial, the care of human poverty, misery, and disease; and these will be wrought out, not by individualism, but by organization and co-operation on a vast scale.

THE GENERAL PROGRESS OF DEMOCRACY

Against the barriers of inherited caste spirit and the biracial character of our population, we must in the next generation convert our Fourth of July democracy into a working social program; must outgrow the feeling that a fixed "lower class" is either necessary or desirable; that an abundant supply of cheap and inefficient labor is an economic advantage; and that education ruins the laboring class, white or black.

We must adopt as our actual working creed the great foundation principle of modern democracy; that the law of human progress is the moral law, as expressed in the Golden

Rule; that no part of the social whole must be sacrificed for the good of another part; that no true liberty is won by enslaving others, and no culture gained by the enforced ignorance of others; that for every citizen high and low there should be a wide-open gate and a free path to that place and plane of service for which his character and abilities fit him.

Such is the inspiring call of the twentieth century to the children of the next generation, to make all the blessings of a Christian civilization the common property of all the people.

America's Call for Lee Leadership

FROM THE cupola of the Washington Building at Washington and Lee University the benignant figure of the glorious Rebel of '76 looks down upon the sacred tomb of his adored kinsman, the later rebel of '61, and guarding the entrance of that most hallowed shrine are bronze statues of those twin rebels, the immortal founders of Washington and Lee.

In the normal development of a nation's life every student of history notes long periods of stability, of crystallized traditions, of dominant conservatism. Then, usually following some tumultuous war, the solid crust is rent asunder as by some volcanic outburst. The ancient landmarks disappear. Long-established standards, creeds, customs, social usages are fused into a fluid magma which will recrystallize in future years into the new forms of a new age.

These periods of swift transition are the turning points in a nation's history, when every passing hour is big with fate and the eternal future is molded on the clanging anvil of the present.

Such a momentous period of post-war reconstruction faced the rebuilders of the desolated South when General Lee began his immortal work at Lexington. His generation faced the mighty task of building a new Southern civilization upon the ruins of the old.

Yet amid the wreckage of all the material possessions of the old South her invisible assets were untouched and undiminished. In that utter midnight of defeat and desolation the

Southern heavens blazed with a constellation of starry virtues never visible, never realized, never possible by day.

Since that tragic era of man-made destruction and heaven-sent heroism two world wars of hellish hatreds and mass murders have wrecked not only the peace and unity but apparently the moral sanity of our world civilization. We are now passing through another period of war-destruction and post-war reconstruction.

Twentieth-century science is destroying many of our ancient religious traditions. War-born vices are undermining our hallowed moral standards. Hysteric nationalism is creating a new form of idolatry. Intoxicating liberty is dissolving our old-time self-restraint. And an epidemic of revolt is assailing every bulwark of authority all around the globe.

The post-war crisis of the wrecked South in 1865 is duplicated all over the United States today. And let me warn every loyal American that it is a far harder task to rebuild shattered morals and religious loyalty than to rebuild shattered bridges and wrecked industries when a nation's courage and character remain unharmed.

What, then, is your imperative duty, your lifelong task, as the present-day makers and leaders of American life and thought? It is to saturate modern science and modern industry with Lee idealism. Make this your supreme effort, your steadfast purpose, your inflexible resolution.

Let me therefore present to you four flashlight pictures of Robert E. Lee as the practical rebuilder of a disintegrated civilization in just such an age as our world is passing through today.

Our first picture is of Lee's inner character, that amazing all-American combination of the rigid morals of the Northern Puritan, the vigorous individuality of the Western pioneer, and the chivalric courtesy of the Southern cavalier.

In him were distilled and concentrated all the ideal virtues of the Old South without its weaknesses. Its unusual combination of manly courage and womanly tenderness, its habitual gentleness toward the weak and helpless, its passionate love of home and children, its lofty sense of personal honor and personal integrity, its chivalrous exaltation of womanhood, its deep fervid religious piety—all these seemed to burst into full flower and perfect fruitage in the character of the South's ideal hero just before the tree of civilization which culminated in such a character was uprooted and destroyed by the tempest of fratricidal war.

Let me urge every true American in this age of war-torn civilization to follow the Lee ideal by adding to the graces of chivalry the sterner and diviner asset of moral self-control.

Our second picture is of Lee as a marvelous example of Christian living during an age specially noted for creedalism and religious partisanship.

His lifetime of service in the regular army was spent in far-off frontier camps, in Mexico during the Mexican War, in countless campaigns, and on scores of battlefields, cut off all the time from the sacred and refining influences of the Christian home, the Christian church, and the weekly Sabbath —that such a military career, in such an environment, should be marked by constant daily prayer, by spotless purity of life and word and conduct, that its dominant passion should be Christian living and spiritual consecration—this is a very miracle of human character transfigured by divine grace.

Thrice fortunate is the South and through her the whole nation that whenever and wherever in the long ages of the future she turns her eyes toward the stately figure of her ideal hero on the pedestal of his ever-growing fame she sees floating over his head, as the one and only flag of his unchanging and eternal allegiance, not the stars and stripes which he so regretfully furled and laid for a time away, nor the stars and bars which disappeared forever amid the smoke and thunder of the battlefield, but the sacred banner of the cross, that star-lit battle flag which knows no North or South, no surrender or defeat, no Gettysburg or Appomattox, that some day, in God's good time, shall float in universal triumph over land and sea all round the world.

My fellow citizens, in these troubled times of world-wide hatreds and restless uncertainty and perplexed bewilderment, my urgent plea is that from General Lee's inspiring example every American leader may realize this important truth, that living, loving, personal faith in a living, loving, personal God is at once the source, the inspiration, aye, and the most accurate measure of all true human greatness.

Our third picture is of Lee, the all-American Progressive, the daring Independent, a half-century ahead not only of his age, but of his family traditions and the very South he fought for. Nothing in his marvelous career is more worthy of imitation and admiration than his far-seeing recognition of the coming future.

You and I live in an age of American science and inventive genius and ever-growing business enterprise. Yet the hands and hearts of our generation are still held fast in hopeless bondage to empty names and ancient fetters and outgrown battle cries. Let the vision of Lee the Progressive inspire every one of you to break every fettering chain whose only warrant is the sanctity of age and unbroken usage.

In that far-off age when the whole South almost deified chattel slavery Lee was an open abolitionist and freed all his personal slaves long before 1861. In an age of religious sectarianism he was always in heart and mind and loyalty an inter-church Christian. In an age of increasing sectionalism and final secesssion he was an open and ardent advocate of an undivided Union. Although a lifelong and professional military leader he openly rejected military discipline in our colleges and universities. Although he fought four years amid the devilish horrors and hatreds of murderous civil war, he never once yielded to war hatred or sectional bitterness, but loved the whole Union even amid the tragedies of utter desolation and defeat.

In an age when King Alcohol reigned supreme, when legal prohibition was hardly dreamed of, when soldiers and sailors were regularly dosed with liquor to increase their battle-ardor—in this age and under these circumstances this regular army officer was always an absolute teetotaler and condemned alcohol in every form and degree as the deadliest enemy of human welfare.

A further example of his marvelous progressiveness was his inner victory over utter defeat. Long since have the slow-moving years crowned as the real victor at Appomattox, not Ulysses S. Grant with his swarming armies, but the immortal and undefeated spirit of Robert Edward Lee.

Surely of all his attributes this daring progressiveness was the most amazing. Rebelling always against political, sectional, and industrial traditionalism, he set you and me and every American a glorious example of courageous independence, of all-American citizenship in a busy present breaking the rusty fetters of an outgrown past.

And this brings me to my fourth and final picture of this forward-looking leader, and I urge every American to duplicate, each in his own environment, General Lee's practical response to the call of the new era.

He was a military son of the Old South, with its ancient system of slave labor, its cultured and masterful oligarchy, its lack of popular education, its exclusive devotion to agriculture—all fatally unfitting it for modern industry. Yet when his starved and ragged heroes surrendered at Appomattox, this lifelong soldier became an educational statesman, the creative engineer of a new industrial South. In five post-bellum years of poverty and wreckage he transformed and developed an ancient classical college into a center of scientific, vocational, and practical training for a new industrial South. He spent his time and energy, not on the classical curriculum of his day, but in training engineers, legislators, journalists, and business experts for new industries and a new era never imagined by his Southern associates.

As twentieth-century Americans, follow his progressive leadership by catching the spirit, attacking the problems, combating the dangers, and thrilling to the possibilities of this marvelous Age of Transition in whose whirlwind activities, on whose far-flung battlefields, your life-conflict is to be won or lost.

Recognize with open mind and open eyes and open heart that this is an age of science and industry yoked in irresistible teamwork. Scientific teamwork and its application to human problems and human activities are transforming our civilization. Let them release our minds from fettering traditions and outgrown ideals and inherited prejudices and hopeless provincialism.

This is the age of the highly trained thinker, of the ardent specialist, of the clear-visioned, warm-hearted expert who can transform pure science and abstract research into human effectiveness and human brotherhood and human welfare.

You face today a whole nation sorely in need of active and effective leadership inspired by Lee effectiveness and consecrated by Lee idealism. Our ancient agricultural tradition, following the Jefferson ideal, glorified individual farm life and tiny general farms. The gullied hillsides, one-horse plows, and ever-present mortgages all over our land bear melancholy witness to the destructive tyranny of this outgrown ideal, so dear to the heart of our fathers. We see around us whole communities of consecrated churchgoers whose Sunday prayers and Sunday sermons and Sunday Bible-study are considered too sacredly religious to be mixed up with week-day votes and party politics and back-street immorality. They have thus become a Pharisaic tradition rather than a vital fellowship with divinity.

Ours is an age of overcrowded schools and colleges. Never have so many Americans been so expensively "educated" as they are today. Yet, alas! never has our blessed land been so filled with daring criminals as it is today. Our courts and jails and penitentiaries are more overcrowded than our colleges.

Surely this world-war age is repeating the novelty and difficulty and perplexity of 1865, and every true American must follow General Lee in responding to the call of the new age.

What comforting truth can we learn from General Lee's swift transition from utter defeat to the leadership of a new era? Surely this—that essentially the things of the spirit are supreme over those of time and sense; that real greatness cannot be determined or measured by the accident of success or failure, but by the in-dwelling spirit with which they are borne; that God-like character may rise triumphant over circumstances however adverse; that our homes and lands, our railways and factories, our visible possessions are not the underlying essentials of American civilization but only its tools and trappings already on their way to the waste-heap.

In concluding my plea for a better America let me not be misunderstood. I have no quarrel with national wealth or national industry or national prosperity. Let the utilization of our national resources continue and increase. Let vast enterprises bear witness to the business ability of our energetic leaders. Let the land echo to the throb of engines and the rattle of machinery. Let the marvels of inventive genius transform every American home. Let every leaping mountain cataract be yoked to the service of man. Let our wide fields grow whiter with fleecy cotton, more golden with ripening grain, more stately with waving corn, smiling back in still more fruitful beauty to the sunny sky above us.

Let the wealth of the world continue to flow in ten thousand channels among our people, till ease and culture and material comfort have lifted the heavy burden of hopeless toil from every American heart and every American home.

But—let the lofty sense of personal honor and personal dignity and personal integrity that distinguished the fathers remain the heritage of their busier sons. Let the old-time chivalry and courtesy and hospitality hold their place in spite of business cares and sordid haste to be rich. Let the scorn of trickery and meanness and the ill-gotten dollar characteristic of the old-time gentlemen of the Lee type protect this younger generation from the many perils of the modern market place. Let the moral and ethical standards of the past prove an effective bulwark against this muddy flood of luxury, frivolity, and shallow mammon-worship.

And above all let the deep and fervid piety of Robert E. Lee and his associates consecrate our growing wealth and power to the service of God and man, purify our politics, our homes, and our ideals, sweeten into loving fraternity the relationship of rich and poor, and thus make our growing wealth and power not only the admiration but the blessing of the whole world.

Thus and thus only shall we be able to yoke the car of our material prosperity to the onrushing chariot wheels of the divine and invisible Purpose,

> And cast in this sublimer mold,
> May the new cycle shame the old!

www.ingramcontent.com/pod-product-compliance
Lightning Source LLC
Chambersburg PA
CBHW021404290426
44108CB00010B/385